POOL
IDEA BOOK

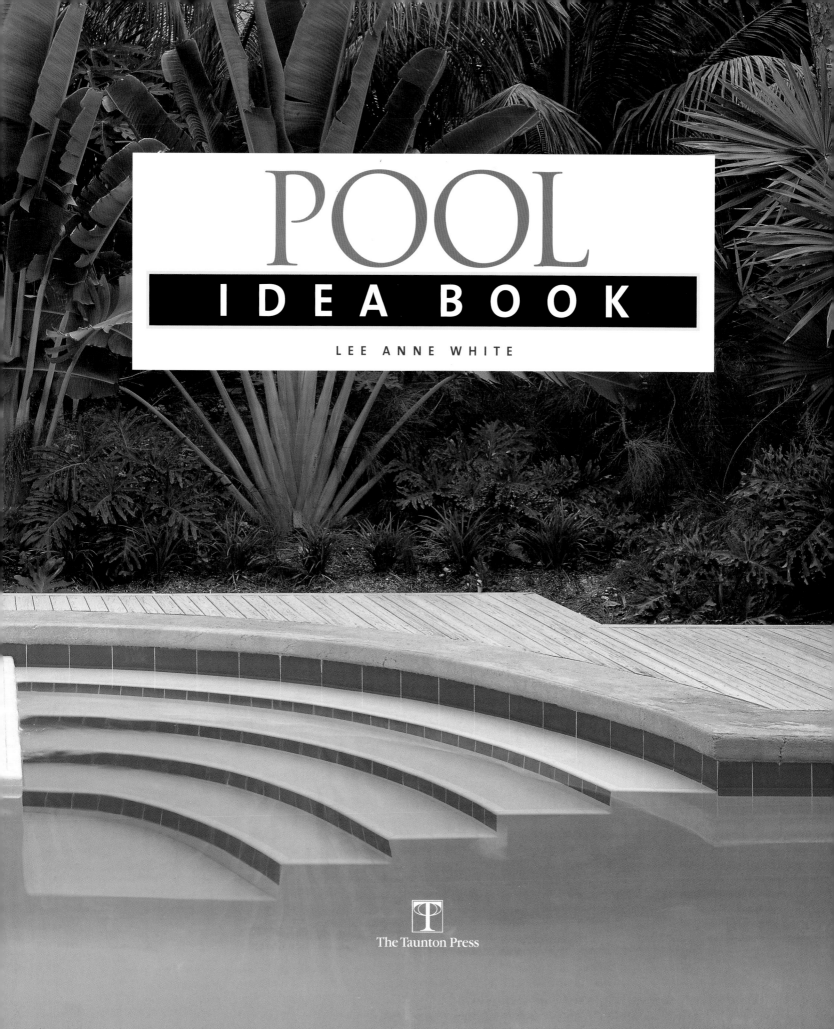

POOL
IDEA BOOK

LEE ANNE WHITE

The Taunton Press

To Dad, for sharing with me his love for the water.

The Taunton Press
Inspiration for hands-on living®

The Taunton Press, Inc., 63 South Main Street, PO Box 5506, Newtown, CT 06470-5506
e-mail: tp@taunton.com

Distributed by Publishers Group West

Editor: Marilyn Zelinsky Syarto
Jacket Design: Jeannet Leendertse
Interior Design: Lori Wendin
Layout: Laura Lind Design
Illustrator: Christine Erikson

Library of Congress Cataloging-in-Publication Data

White, Lee Anne.
  Pool idea book / Lee Anne White.
     p. cm.
  ISBN 1-56158-665-X
 1. Swimming pools. I. Title: Pool idea book. II. Title.
TH4763.W45 2004
728'.962--dc22

                              2003022745

Printed in Singapore
10 9 8 7 6 5 4 3 2 1

Acknowledgments

I would like to acknowledge and thank the many landscape architects, pool builders, interior designers, manufacturers, and organizations who assisted me in the research and development of this book—especially Betty Ajay, Chuck Baldwin, Ron Coker, Sr., Michelle Derviss, David Ellis, Mike Farley, Brad McGill, Richard McPherson, Jennifer Romberg, Michael Thilgen, David Thorne, Paula Refi, Jeni Webber, and the National Spa & Pool Institute.

Special thanks to the homeowners, designers, and pool builders who shared their pools with us; the photographers who captured the spirit of these places on film; landscape architects—including Thomas Church and Isabelle Greene—who inspired us to think in new ways about swimming pools and their role in the landscape; and the talented team of editors and designers at The Taunton Press.

And finally, a personal note of appreciation to Sydney Eddison and Jeni Webber for their unending support; to John Lively, who gave me my shot in the publishing world; and to my husband, Alan White, with whom I look forward to sharing many sunny afternoons around our pool.

Contents

Introduction ▪ 2

Chapter 1
New Choices for Pools and Spas ▪ 4

Architectural Pools ▪ 6

Naturalistic Pools ▪ 16

Lap Pools ▪ 22

Recreational Pools ▪ 28

Aboveground Pools ▪ 36

Spas ▪ 38

Chapter 2
In and around the Pool ▪ 44

Inside the Pool ▪ 46

The Pool's Edge ▪ 54

The Pool Deck ▪ 64

Chapter 3

Landscaping Your Pool · 82

Positioning Your Pool · 84

Show Your Style · 90

Enclosing the Pool · 96

Poolside Plantings · 106

Lighting for Safety and Pleasure · 126

Chapter 4

Outdoor Rooms and Structures · 130

Gathering Spaces · 132

Poolhouses · 152

Equipment Rooms · 164

Resources · 168

Credits · 169

Introduction

Swimming is one of the most popular recreational activities in America, but you don't necessarily have to be a swimmer to enjoy a pool. In fact, you can benefit from the cooling, relaxing effects of a pool in the landscape even if your favorite activity is sitting by the edge of the pool in a comfortable lounge chair. With the addition of a swimming pool, you can create an inviting oasis in your own backyard—a place to escape not only the heat but also the stresses of everyday living.

Once just a rectangular hole in the ground surrounded by an apron of concrete, today's swimming pools come in myriad shapes and styles suited to backyards of just about any size. They can be as simple as a small, square wading pool or a long, rectangular lap pool, or as elaborate as a naturalistic pool with a cascading waterfall, sandy beach, and boulders. Innovative features such as vanishing edges, fountains, underwater benches, and fiber optic lighting have turned swimming pools into dramatic focal points in the landscape. Pool decks are as likely to be covered in stone, brick, or tile as in concrete—which, these days, can be stained, stamped, or textured to look like just about anything *except* concrete. Even spas, whether for

physical therapy or simple relaxation, can be integrated into a pool, placed on a deck near the bedroom, or transformed into a dramatic water feature.

As the lines between indoor and outdoor living are blurred, swimming pools are quickly becoming the centerpieces for outdoor living. Patios, pavilions, and poolhouses make it a pleasure to gather around the pool with family and friends. Multipurpose grills and outdoor kitchen islands have brought alfresco dining to a new level of convenience. Stylish, durable, all-weather tables, chairs, and outdoor decor have changed the way we furnish our pool decks and patios. The availability of exterior fireplaces and landscape lighting have extended both the hours and seasons we can spend around the pool.

The recent advances in pool construction techniques mean that there is much more to swimming pool design than selecting an image from a catalog. In many cases, you'll want to hire an architect, landscape architect, or professional pool designer to assist with the process. However, with more than 300 photographs and drawings, we hope *Taunton's Pool Idea Book* will get you off to a great start by offering a visual feast of innovative ideas for designing the ultimate poolscape for any budget, space, or lifestyle.

This book will help you sort through the options for designing pools and spas—to make informed decisions that will increase the value of your pool and enhance any backyard setting. It will also help you evaluate and plan the surrounding structures, outdoor rooms, and landscape—to build a safe haven for outdoor activities and to create unity between your pool and home. Most of all, we hope this book will inspire you to create an environment in which you, your family, and your friends will spend many long, enjoyable summers relaxing around the pool.

New Choices for Pools and Spas

In the past, all pools looked pretty much the same. That's not the case anymore. Today's pools run the gamut from pint-size plunge pools to competition-length lap pools, round reflecting pools to free-form recreational pools, and striking architectural pools with vanishing edges to naturalistic pools edged with boulders, waterfalls, and lush plantings. Pools can be designed to fit almost any budget, suit just about any size lot, and complement most architectural styles. They can be built indoors or out, with or without a spa, and accented with an amazing array of add-on features—from fountains and cascades to beaches, underwater benches, and massaging jets. What was once just "the old swimming hole" now has the power to transform a backyard into a private retreat.

With so many choices in pool and spa design, it's important to carefully evaluate your needs and desires before taking the plunge into swimming pool ownership. The location, shape, size, depth, and features of your pool are all determined by how you want to use it—whether for exercise, recreation or relaxation—and what role you expect it to play in your landscape. Before contacting a pool builder, consider the interests of individual family members and assess how your needs may change over time. It's easier and much more affordable to make changes during the planning process than it is once construction has begun.

◄ A WELL-DESIGNED POOL ENHANCES THE LANDSCAPE AND MAKES THE BACKYARD A PRIZED DESTINATION FOR HOMEOWNERS and guests alike. This naturalistic pool is the focal point of the landscape. The lush plantings and boulders around the pool and storage shed make this an ideal retreat or a perfect spot for entertaining.

Architectural Pools

A N ARCHITECTURAL POOL IS A CUSTOM-BUILT SWIMMING POOL that has been designed in such a way that it has an undeniable relationship with the accompanying house. At times, it may even be difficult to distinguish where the house ends and the pool begins. More often, however, the house and pool are separate and distinct elements that relate to one another through their alignment and use of construction materials. On occasion, the pool itself is a striking architectural element in the landscape, with strong lines and bold geometric shapes. For these reasons, it's not surprising that architectural pools are frequently designed by architects and constructed at the same time as the house.

Architectural pools are typically placed close to the house, with a pool deck or terrace doubling as a transitional space between the two. Paving materials may flow from indoor rooms out onto the pool deck, and large expanses of windows may overlook the pool area.

▼ MODULAR SHAPES, CLEAN LINES, AND SIMPLE materials are used in the design and construction of both this house and pool. They are further united by a transitional deck, which extends from the walls of the house all the way to the pool's edge.

◄ BY PAYING CLOSE ATTENTION TO details, even a small pool can make a strong architectural statement in the landscape. This one is raised to a comfortable seating height and accented by a raised deck. The bold color contrast between the pool's interior and its surrounds is also eye-catching.

▶ THE REPETITION OF CIRCULAR elements lends this landscape a sense of formality and intrigue. Circles can be found in the pool itself, the spa, the steps leading into the pool, and the brick retaining walls that surround the pool and spa.

Budgeting Basics

BUILDING A POOL is like remodeling or adding a new room onto your house. Industry experts suggest budgeting around 15 percent of your total property value on the pool and surrounding landscape, or as much as 20 percent if you include a poolhouse or other special features. If your property is valued at $300,000, you can expect to spend around $45,000 on an in-ground pool and landscaping.

▲ IN CONTRAST TO THE UNUSUAL, sloping angles of the roofline, the rest of the house speaks to a sense of simplicity in its overall design, materials, and landscaping. The simplicity of the pool, deck, and plantings echoes the design of the house. Yet, like the roofline, the pool sits at an angle to the house to give the composition of the backyard an element of surprise.

THIS POOL WAS BUILT WHERE A COURTYARD WOULD TRADITIONALLY BE located. As a result, it can be viewed from several surrounding rooms through floor-to-ceiling windows and sliding-glass doors. A breezeway connects these rooms by passing over the water like a bridge.

THE OWNER OF THIS POOL STARTED with a simple rectangular design and then altered it on each side with nooks and crannies to create a distinctive design. The tiered, aboveground decking makes the pool site architecturally interesting and offers additional places to entertain.

▲ AN IRREGULARLY SHAPED POOL RADIATES out from this house. The wide steps descend from the back terrace and continue into the pool, creating continuity between the deck, steps, and pool.

▶ THE STONE-AND-CONCRETE FOUNDATION of this house doubles as an interior wall for the pool. Bringing the water this close to the house creates a stunning view through the floor-to-ceiling windows, while water casts reflections on the interior walls of the house, creating a sense of light and movement throughout the day.

Who Designs Pools?

Architects, landscape architects, landscape designers, and pool builders all design pools. Consult an architect if you are building both a house and a pool, adding a poolhouse, or if your site poses unusual engineering challenges. A landscape architect or landscape designer can help design a pool that blends with an existing home, as well as design the surrounding landscape. Many pool builders have architects or landscape architects on staff that can design custom pools; others offer off-the-shelf plans that may better suit a limited budget.

▼ DOUBLE DECKS CREATE GATHERING PLACES BESIDE this pool. The upper deck serves as a transitional space, while the lower deck provides a platform from which to enter and exit the pool. The rectangular pattern in the deck tiles and windows ties it all together.

FOUNTAINS AND CASCADES

▽ BY PLACING A WATER FEATURE NEAR
the house, its gentle, soothing
sounds can be enjoyed both
indoors and around the pool.
A sheet waterfall has been placed
beneath this bedroom window,
where it helps the homeowners
ease into a good night's sleep.

▷ FIBER OPTIC LIGHTS ILLUMINATE THESE
arching jets of water, while a
computer-controlled color wheel
automatically changes their color,
creating a theatrical poolside perfor-
mance. Laminar-flow jets, which
create the arches, are positioned
away from the pool so that the
water shoots up and over the pool
deck and into the water.

▷ THOUGH THE HIGH MASONRY WALL buffers some sound, it is more effective as a privacy wall and windscreen. Splashing water does a much better job of masking the surrounding neighborhood noise. A generous flow of water pours through flumes, churning into the lap pool below.

◁ WATER APPEARS TO CASCADE OVER THE DAM OF A SMALL canal, but closer inspection reveals that water is actually forced through a series of small holes, creating a sheet waterfall that flows into a naturalistic pool.

The Sound of Water

RUNNING WATER is one of the most relaxing sounds in any landscape—which is why water features in pools are so popular. Of course, all types of running water do not sound the same. You can achieve the desired sound effect by adjusting the volume of water, the distance that it falls, and the surface over which it falls. A rule of thumb: The greater the volume of water and the greater the distance it falls, the louder the sound it makes.

The Water-Wise Pool

WATER HAS BECOME a scarce resource in many fast-growing communities and regions with limited rainfall. As a result, some municipalities have placed restrictions on water use for pools. To cooperate with water-conservation practices, build your pool only as large and as deep as needed for anticipated activities and don't automatically empty your pool at the end of the season. In most cases, water can be left in pools over the winter, even in cold climates.

◀ SPRAY-JET NOZZLES CAN CREATE a variety of fountain effects. Streaming jets, like this one, can produce single or multiple streams of water at varied heights. Fanning jets produce a clear sheet of water that is best suited to sheltered, windless sites.

▶ WATER MOVES MORE SLOWLY AND MAKES less noise when entering this pool after traveling down a rough, sloping, split-rock surface than it would cascading through a flume or over a straight ledge. However, the slow trickle of water can be as hypnotic in sight and sound as a crashing cascade.

▲ THE STEPS LEADING INTO THIS POOL double as a waterfall. There's no need to worry about slippery stone steps because the pool's chlorinated water prevents the buildup of algae.

◄ WATER SPILLS CONTINUOUSLY FROM the spa into the pool below through a narrow cutout. It has a distinctive sound, like that of water being poured from a bucket into a pool of water.

Naturalistic Pools

IN CONTRAST TO THE STRONG LINES OF AN ARCHITECTURAL POOL, a naturalistic swimming pool is designed to blend almost seamlessly into its surrounding landscape. It is commonly placed at a greater distance from the house, often along a woodland edge or at a low point where you might expect to find a pond. In fact, most naturalistic pools mimic ponds or lagoons in their free-form shape, and they are often enhanced with trickling streams and cascading waterfalls. The pool's edges may be anchored with boulders and planting pockets, or they may descend gradually down into the water from dry land, resembling a sandy beach.

◄ WITH NO SIGN OF ANY MANMADE EDGES, THIS SMALL pool looks like a natural spring. The stepping-stones and lush carpet of soft, creeping ground covers enhance the woodland setting.

▼ THE ABUNDANT BOULDERS CREATE A NATURALISTIC environment around this free-form pool. The random stone paving, recirculating stream, and garden paths help create a natural-looking setting.

◀ DESIGNED IN THE 1970S BY RENOWNED landscape architect Thomas Church, this pool was among the first naturalistic swimming pools. The dark bottom allows the boulders and grasses tucked around the pool's edges to be reflected in the water.

▲ ALTHOUGH THIS OVAL POOL HAS A MORTARED, CUT-STONE EDGE, ITS small size, its position at the bottom of a hill under the shade of trees, and the surrounding landscape all work together to create the appearance of a small pond.

Before You Dig

BUILDING A SWIMMING POOL requires construction—an activity that almost always interests local officials, utility companies, and neighbors. Before you break ground, check your zoning laws, building codes, health and safety codes, property deed, and subdivision covenants for any restrictions, easements, setbacks, or safety requirements. Identify the location of any septic tanks, rock ledges, and underground utilities that could affect where you place your pool, and make absolutely sure that this information is relayed to your pool designer and builder.

▼ THE WOODLAND, WHICH IS VIEWED THROUGH THE ARBOR, creates a natural backdrop for this pool. The concrete decking faces the lawn and the house and creates a subtle transition from the manmade poolscape to the natural landscape beyond.

▼ DENSE PLANTINGS OBSCURE A WOODEN FENCE, transforming this space into a naturalistic setting. Paths wind naturally around planting pockets near the pool's edge.

◄ THIS POOL LOOKS LIKE A LAGOON. The effect is achieved with a freeform shape, a natural-looking edge, a textured bottom resembling sand, turquoise water reflecting off the pool's interior, and tropical plantings. A hammock strung between palm trees adds an appropriate finishing touch to the setting.

▲ THE POOL, POSITIONED AT THE rear of the property, along the woodland edge, beckons guests as they catch a glance of it from inside the house. Because it is placed at a distance from the house, the pool becomes the prime—and much anticipated— destination of the backyard.

Recycling Excavated Soil

WHEN INSTALLING an in-ground pool, your contractors will have to remove many truckloads of soil. Rather than pay to have the soil hauled off, consider using it elsewhere in your landscape to create rolling terrain or mounds, which are especially appropriate around a naturalistic pool or spa. You can use mounds in the design of waterfalls and gently falling streams as well as to plant raised wind buffers and screening.

FALLING WATER

▲ THE STEEP SLOPE OF THIS SITE PROVIDED THE
homeowners with an opportunity to design
a series of small pools with a waterfall. The
waterfall spills into a small pond adjacent to,
but separate from, the swim area and spa.
Each pool has tile edging for seating.

▲ ONE OF THE KEYS TO MAKING A RECIRCULATING WATERFALL LOOK NATURAL IS
camouflaging the water's origin. Dense, fast-growing ornamental
grasses do the trick here.

◄ A WELL-POSITIONED SPOTLIGHT ILLUMINATES THIS SPA'S WATERFALL AT NIGHT.
The water cascades down four steps, making the homeowners feel as
though they are enjoying a dip in a secluded mountain hot spring.

▶ THE ROUGH-CUT EDGES OF STACKED STONES HAVE AN APPEALING, AGED LOOK,
even when newly installed. The cascading water and therapeutic spa
make this setting even more inviting.

▶ A GRADE CHANGE, WHETHER A NATURAL HILLSIDE OR A MANMADE MOUND, is essential for creating a waterfall, while boulders help hold the soil in place. The bottom third of these boulders was buried so that they appear natural in the landscape.

Artificial Stone

REMOVING STONES and boulders from the landscape to place around the pool is not only a labor-intensive and expensive job, but it also often leaves behind environmental problems, such as erosion or the altered flow of rivers where rocks are removed. Artificial stone is an environmentally friendly and less expensive alternative to the real thing, and because artificial stones are lightweight, they are much easier to move into place around a pool. A good craftsman can make faux-stone boulders look and feel real to the touch.

Lap Pools

SWIMMING IS AN EXCELLENT LOW-IMPACT AEROBIC EXERCISE, as mentally relaxing as it is physically invigorating. For those who desire a pool for fitness purposes, lap pools are an excellent option. Efficient in size and suitable to most lots, lap pools holds less water than most recreational pools and, because of their simple design—little more than a long, narrow lane for swimming—complement almost any architectural style. Any lap pool that is 40 to 75 ft. long, 8 to 10 ft. wide, and at least 3½ ft. deep should satisfy most swimmers. For those who want to do more than swim laps, an unobstructed swimming lane can be designated in a larger recreational pool.

◄ A COVERED POOL ALLOWS FOR swimming, rain or shine. The open sides of the structure allow fresh air to circulate. This single-lane lap pool features steps built into the side and a ladder for easy exits. Nearby closets conceal the pool equipment.

▲ THIS L-SHAPED LAP POOL OFFERS THE
best of both worlds: a long lane
for swimming plus a wider area for
recreation that is suitable for water
sports and relaxing on floats.

Steps for Lap Pools

FOR SAFETY AND CONVENIENCE, the steps in a lap pool should be designed so that they do not interfere with swimming. The walls at the ends of the lane should remain flat and parallel to accommodate flip turns. In a narrow, single-lane lap pool, the ladder should be recessed into the sidewall, with a handrail built into the deck for support. In a wider lap pool, narrow steps can be placed along one side—just mark both the swimming lane and steps with paint or tile to help swimmers stay on course. You can also extend a section of the pool to accommodate steps. In fact, these extensions add a decorative element to an otherwise simple pool design. When a lap pool is part of a larger, multipurpose pool, build steps and ladders away from the lanes.

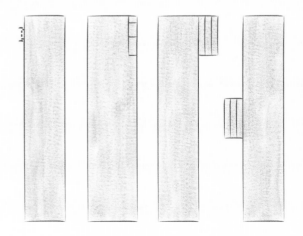

◀ THE OWNERS OF THIS SHALLOW LOT made excellent use of their space by tucking in a long, narrow lap pool. Steps are placed near both ends for convenience.

▼ ONE OF THE CHARMS OF LAP POOLS is their simple design. Most are long and linear, such as this pool, which makes a strong visual statement in the landscape. It accentuates the linearity of this outdoor room.

▼ THE DESIGNER OF THIS LAP POOL CREATED AN EXTENSION on one side so the steps would be out of the swim lanes. Such extensions can also be placed at the center of one side of a lap pool or designed as semi-circular spaces rather than rectangles.

Swim Spas

A SWIM SPA CAN PROVIDE A COMPACT ALTERNATIVE to a lap pool. Swim spas—sometimes called jet pools—are small pools with adjustable water jets that create a current and allow you to swim in place—much like jogging on a treadmill. By adjusting these jets, you can increase the intensity of your workout and accommodate swimmers with different skill, endurance, and strength levels.

Many swim spas double as spas with massaging hydro-jets. Allow enough time for the water to heat up or cool down between activities. The ideal water temperature is 78°F to 82°F for swimming and 98°F to 104°F for hydrotherapy. An alternative is to build a swim spa with two areas—one for swimming and one for relaxing—each with its own temperature control.

Swim spas occupy much less space and use less water than lap pools, yet are larger than most spas. They average 13 to 20 ft. long and can be easily tucked into even the tiniest of backyards. Most are 3½ to 4 ft. deep, but deeper models are available for water aerobics.

▲ LIKE OTHER TYPES OF POOL, SWIM SPAS ARE AVAILABLE IN ASSORTED SHAPES AND SIZES.
Spas are smaller and easier to tuck into a hillside than a full-size pool. This kidney-shaped swim spa fits naturally into a sloped yard that overlooks a nearby lake.

◄ A SLEEK INDOOR LAP POOL RUNS ALONG ONE SIDE of the house. Because this pool is designed for exercise rather than for sunbathing or entertaining, the deck width was kept to a minimum. Sliding doors open to let in fresh air, and closets are handy for storing pool gear.

▲ THESE HOMEOWNERS ENJOY SWIMMING YEAR-round with an indoor pool. The skylights and large windows offer natural lighting to help bring the outdoors in, while upstairs windows create a dramatic view and allow the home-owners to keep an eye on poolside activities.

 LARGE WINDOWS AND TWO SKYLIGHTS provide ample light. Although the room is painted bright white, the unusual angles of the walls, windows, and pool give the space plenty of architectural interest.

◀ THIS RECTANGULAR LAP POOL has a spa on one end, which helps enhance the getaway atmosphere created by the building's log-cabin-style construction. Durable blue-stone decking frames the entire space.

Recreational Pools

THE MOST POPULAR POOLS ARE THOSE DESIGNED FOR A VARIETY of recreational activities—from floating and swimming to water volleyball and diving. Recreational pools can be built in any shape, size, or style and often include coves for wading or for children's play. Although most recreational pools are 3½ ft. to 5 ft. deep, the depth of a pool can vary from one end to the other. For diving, one end of the pool should be at least 11 ft. deep. For games and water aerobics, a 4-ft.-deep area is ideal for keeping everyone's heads above water. Special features, such as waterfalls, slides, and underwater benches, make hanging out by the pool a favorite family pastime.

▼ THIS KIDNEY-SHAPED RECREATIONAL pool is small enough to tuck into a side yard on a sloped lot with room to spare for brick decking and poolside planting pockets.

◄ CAREFUL MAINTENANCE CAN EXTEND THE LIFE OF A VINYL
liner. This one lasted for 20 years before it had to be replaced. The broad end of this lazy-L-shaped pool is 11 ft. deep, which is considered a safe depth for diving.

▶ A BROAD DECK ON ONE SIDE OF THIS RECTANGULAR pool offers plenty of space for lounge chairs and tables. With the surrounding lush gardens enhancing the setting, this pool area also serves as a cool, restful spot for entertaining.

Building an In-Ground Pool

IN-GROUND POOLS COME IN THREE BASIC construction types: concrete, vinyl-lined, and fiberglass. A concrete pool—whether poured, gunite, shotcrete, or masonry block—is highly durable, can be built in almost any shape or size imaginable, and can be finished in a wide variety of colors, textures, or tiled patterns. A vinyl-lined or fiberglass pool—although limited in shape, size, and finish—costs less, can be installed quickly, and provides a good alternative for cold climates where a concrete pool could crack without special reinforcement.

▼ THIS POOL COULD BE DESIGNED IN ANY SHAPE IMAGINED BY THE homeowners because a custom frame was built on site and then filled with concrete. In contrast, vinyl-lined or fiberglass pools are typically offered in a limited range of shapes and sizes.

▼ A DIVING BOARD OFFERS HOURS of enjoyment for swimmers. For safety, diving boards should extend out over deep water and be located away from slides, steps, and other recreational equipment.

◀ THIS MULTIFUNCTIONAL POOL
features several activity areas, along with an underwater bench on the right side. Plantings provide shady relief for swimmers who prefer to stay in the water but need a short rest from the rays.

▼ LOCATED AWAY FROM THE HOUSE
and down a flight of stone steps, as part of a garden, this pool is designed as a destination area. A multitude of gathering spaces are offered, both in and out of water. Shallow steps that run the width of one end of the pool and an underwater bench on the right side of the pool offer ample in-the-water seating.

Dive Safely

DESPITE GROWING SAFETY CONCERNS, diving is still a popular swimming pool activity. The keys to diving safely include having plenty of deep-water pool area and proper supervision. Though standards vary, safety organizations recommend at least 11 ft. of water beneath the board, with the deep end extending at least 16 ft. from the board into the middle of the pool. Short jump boards, which offer limited spring, and fixed-platform diving rocks are gaining in popularity over traditional, longer diving boards.

Updating Existing Pools

A NY POOL CAN BE UPGRADED, though major changes—such as converting from a vinyl-lined pool to a concrete one—can cost as much as installing a new pool. To refresh your pool, consider expanding or resurfacing the deck, changing the coping around the pool's edge, updating the interior finish, or adding special features such as spas, waterfalls, fountains, and swim-up bars. Other options for enhancing your poolside setting include arbors, pool-houses, or outdoor kitchens.

▲ SUNBATHING IS A PRIORITY AROUND this pool. In addition to the chaise lounges, the convex spaces at each end of the pool increase the room for floats. The lush green grass gives swimmers' feet cooling relief.

◀ THIS POOL GENTLY WRAPS AROUND the corner of the house, leaving plenty of room for an exuberant garden. The proximity of the pool to the house increases the homeowners' use of the space, whether for swimming or outdoor entertaining.

▲ THIS BACKYARD IS A GATHERING space with the swimming pool as the focal point. The boulders and naturalistic plantings set the mood for hours of entertaining in nature.

Shaped to Suit Your Style

IF YOU CAN IMAGINE A POOL SHAPE, someone can build it. So how do you settle on a shape? The layout of your house or shape of your lot is often the driving factor behind choosing a pool design. Your setting is important, too. Pools with geometric shapes tend to suit traditional homes and landscapes, while free-form pools are called for in more casual settings. Rectangular pools, still a popular option, support a wide range of activities and are easily equipped with automatic covers. But in the end, it's often a simple matter of personal preference.

COMMON POOL SHAPES

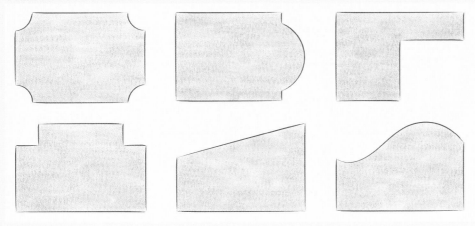

SMALL POOLS

◀ THE SMALLER THE LOT, THE SIMPLER
the shape of the pool should be.
The homeowner of this tiny yard
and pool created an inviting,
intimate setting by cultivating
tall garden walls and planting
lush greenery.

▼ IMAGINE TAKING AN AFTERNOON
walk and stumbling upon this
perfectly round pool set against a
natural hillside. Because the homeowners designed the area to be a
quiet retreat rather than a recreational spot, they eliminated the
need for a traditional pool deck.

Take the Plunge

PLUNGE POOLS—small, shallow pools intended for lounging rather than for swimming—are growing in popularity due to their lower cost, smaller size, and reduced water needs. Especially suited to a small site, plunge pools can also be tucked into small corners on larger lots. Because plunge pools are small, it is often possible to upgrade the materials or add a water feature without exceeding your budget.

▲ THIS SMALL POOL DOES DOUBLE duty as a garden feature. The oval design, which helps the pool blend into the surrounding formal landscape, provides a place to cool off during a hot summer afternoon.

▶ THIS PINT-SIZE POOL PACKS A LOT of impact. It contains an elevated spa, multiple waterfalls, and an underwater bench. A small, raised lawn for sunbathing overlooks the pool. The brick steps and walls connect the pool to the house, which is built from the same material.

▼ IN FENCED BACKYARDS, SHALLOW ABOVEGROUND POOLS can be subtly screened with the strategic placement of loose shrubbery, clipped hedges, and other plantings. The low-growing shrubs surrounding this pool camouflage the pool's base while still offering clear views of the pool for safety.

▲ THE WHITE FENCING AND WHITE OUTDOOR FURNITURE GIVE A sense of unity to this white-edged pool. The interior steps and safety railing are also white. Decking surrounds the pool, making it feel more like an in-ground pool and offering plenty of space for gathering and sunbathing.

Aboveground Advantages

◄ THOUGH MOST ABOVEGROUND POOLS ARE MADE OF METAL, this one features a wooden exterior that is as attractive as it is functional. It also features a small deck for seating and pool access.

▼ A SLOPED SITE CAN ACCOMODATE AN ABOVE-GROUND pool when the land is minimally graded to create a level base. If the pool is positioned so that the upside rim is only slightly above ground level, decking can create the illusion of an in-ground pool.

A N ABOVEGROUND POOL offers several advantages over an in-ground pool. The most significant consideration is its substantially lower price tag. For this reason, many homeowners try out an aboveground pool before investing in a permanent, in-ground pool. An aboveground pool can be constructed in a matter of days, instead of the weeks required to build an in-ground pool. It is also a good choice for rocky landscapes where excavation can be difficult. Because many are portable, some homeowners take their aboveground pools with them when they move.

Spas

SPAS HAVE COME A LONG WAY FROM THE WOODEN-BARREL HOT TUBS OF THE 1960s, but soaking in hot water still offers the same benefits: relaxation, improved circulation, and relief for tired, aching muscles. In addition to hot tubs, choices include portable and prefabricated spas, as well as in-ground, concrete spas. Today's spas feature flexible seating arrangements, high-pressure massaging jets, and computerized temperature controls. A few even come with their own sound systems. A spa can be designed as a stand-alone unit or integrated with a pool to take advantage of shared water and filtration systems. To reap the greatest benefits of a spa, keep the water temperature between 99°F and 104°F.

▼ THIS GENTLY SLOPING SITE ENABLED THE spa to be placed so that it overlooks the pool. When working on a sloped site, it's important to consider how raised decks or retaining walls might be used as jumping platforms by swimmers, and to either place them further from the pool or increase the pool depth accordingly.

CONCRETE SPAS, SUCH AS THIS crescent-shaped one, offer the greatest design flexibility because custom forms allow the concrete to be shaped in any number of ways. Prefabricated spas, while limited in shape and size, tend to feature more comfortable seating.

SPAS CAN BE PLACED EITHER ABOVE OR IN THE GROUND. THIS aboveground spa has a wide rim that doubles as a seating area and can be used as a resting place for towels and amenities.

A SPA PLACED ADJACENT TO A POOL DOESN'T TAKE UP INTERIOR POOL space but can still share a water-circulation system.

▲ THE HOMEOWNERS PLACED THIS SPA A SHORT DASH FROM indoors so they could kick back in the warm water on chilly evenings. Potted plants sit safely along the spa's rim.

▶ THIS SQUARE SPA IS LOCATED NEAR the house where it benefits from increased privacy. The home's walls also buffer chilling winds during evening soaks. The dark stone rim absorbs heat from the sun for a warm, comfortable seating area.

▶ A NOOK WAS CREATED FOR THIS SPA in a corner next to the pool and cabana where it offers greater privacy and feels more intimate nestled between two columns.

▽ ALTHOUGH THE POOL AND SPA ARE not physically connected, they still share a water-circulation system. Visually, the pool, spa, and landscape are united through the repetition of circular design elements, including the round dish that aids in the flow of water between the spa and pool.

Custom Jets

HEAT AND HYDRAULICS make a hot tub or spa inviting, whether you're just looking to relax or are seeking a therapeutic massage. Today's spas come with elaborate jet systems—often dozens of jets, strategically placed for a neck-to-toe body massage. Many newer models enable you to control the jets individually, adjusting the flow or pressure for optimum comfort.

▼ THIS PORTABLE SPA IS PLACED ON A DECK WHERE it is easily accessible year-round. Before placing a spa on a deck or porch, make sure structural beams are reinforced for the extra load.

▲ ALTHOUGH THIS SPA IS ADJACENT TO AND INTEGRATED into the shape of the pool, the circulation systems are separate. Separate systems are more efficient if the pool is not heated or is closed for much of the year.

▶ THIS SPA IS SET WITHIN THE POOL'S BOUNDARY AND slightly below the water level of the pool so the homeowners can use a single automatic pool cover. Covering a spa when it is not in use reduces heat loss and evaporation.

◄ PREFABRICATED SPAS OFFER
comfortable, anatomically designed seating arrangements. The homeowners cleverly integrated this spa into the rugged landscape by adding a raised stone deck and wall, along with an arbor and ample plantings.

Energy Efficiency

Heaters are a part of every spa system, and optional heaters can extend your season in the swimming pool. Heaters, however, can also run up your utility bill. Many solar heating systems are available, and all can help decrease your utility costs. When designing a pool, keep in mind that a shallow pool heats up more quickly than a deep pool, and that pools can be positioned for maximum sun exposure. If a pool site is exposed to winds, install windbreaks to reduce both water evaporation and wind chill.

◄ THIS SPA WAS PLACED IN AN OPEN AREA BETWEEN THE main house and guesthouse and screened with ornamental grasses for privacy. It offers excellent star-gazing potential.

In and around the Pool

A pool's interior is an often-overlooked aspect of pool design. But the size and placement of underwater features such as steps, benches, and wading areas often influence how you use your pool and how much time you spend in the water. In addition, the interior surface—whether vinyl, plaster, paint, tile, aggregate, or fiberglass—greatly affects a pool's appearance, durability, and maintenance requirements.

Although the pool may be the center of attention, what surrounds it goes a long way toward setting the stage for an enjoyable afternoon in the sun. Adjacent decks are primarily for poolside activities: sunbathing, entertaining, or just relaxing while the kids swim. Pool decks are also transitional spaces—and you need plenty of room to move around, even after adding a few large chaise lounges. Decks have another key role, too—that of uniting the pool with the house through the use of matching or complementary construction materials.

◀ THE CONTRASTING MEDIUM-DARK COPING AGAINST A LIGHT DECKING MATERIAL MAKES THE POOL THE CENTER OF ATTENTION in this backyard—even though it is surrounded by several large structures. Clustered terra-cotta containers echo the color and texture of the tile coping.

Inside the Pool

INTERIOR FINISHES ARE AS VARIED AS POOL STYLES AND SHAPES. They come in myriad patterns, colors, and textures. Materials—from vinyl and fiberglass to concrete covered with plaster, paint, aggregate, or tile—also vary in cost, durability, and ease of upkeep. Regardless of the material, a pool's finish should be attractive, nonslippery, watertight, durable, and easily cleaned.

Of course, a pool's interior includes more than just the finish. You must also consider its depth and features. You'll appreciate steps for their convenience over ladders and gravitate toward sitting areas, such as underwater benches, stools, broad steps, and shallow wading areas.

▼ A WHITE PLASTER POOL FINISH, WHICH makes pool water appear pale blue when it reflects the sky, is a good choice for warm climates and shallow pools because it keeps the water from getting too warm in the heat of summer. However, dirt and debris on the pool bottom show up more easily in a light-colored pool.

◀ USING TILE CAN CREATE DRAMATIC patterns both inside and around pools. The refracting quality of water accentuates the patterns that tile makes—especially when the water in the pool is moving.

▲ THE COLORING PIGMENT IN BLACK PLASTER TENDS TO MOTTLE over time. While this look enhances naturalistic pools, it can be distracting in more traditional pools. Choose a dark gray plaster finish for a more uniform appearance that will still have strong reflecting characteristics.

True Colors

"WATER COLOR" is a term that actually refers to a combination of the pool's interior finish and the reflected sky—after all, water is clear. With the sky as a factor, a pool's color can even shift slightly during the day. In general, white pool finishes make the water appear pale blue, and dark gray pool finishes create a black appearance. A pool designer can help you select a plaster, paint, or pebble finish to attain various shades of blue, green, or gray.

Finishing Touches

POOL FINISHES VARY GREATLY, **not only in color and texture but also in durability, ease of maintenance, and cost. Here's a brief comparison of the most common options:**

- **Vinyl liners** are available in many colors and patterns. They are affordable and can be installed quickly over both structural pool walls and a sand base. Even if cared for properly, vinyl liners must be replaced every 10 to 15 years. Sharp objects can tear holes in a vinyl liner.
- **Fiberglass** pools are impervious to sharp objects and are slightly textured. Although they are usually delivered to a site as finished pool shells, recent technological developments now allow fiberglass pools to be built on-site.
- **Plaster** is the most traditional finish for concrete pools. It comes in a variety of colors and creates a long-lasting finish. Its textured surface, however, can be difficult to clean and stains easily.
- **Stone aggregate** offers a natural-looking finish. The tiny stone particles create a durable, textured finish that hides dirt between regular cleanings.
- **Paint** is a less expensive finish than plaster. It is available in many colors and creates a hard, impervious surface. However, pools must be repainted every five years or so with a specially formulated paint to maintain durability.
- **Tile** is the most costly pool finish, but it is available in the greatest range of styles and colors. It is also extremely durable and easy to clean. Decorative patterns and mosaics of tile can dress up a pool's interior. Though pool tile may be glazed or nonglazed, it should be dense and impervious to water.

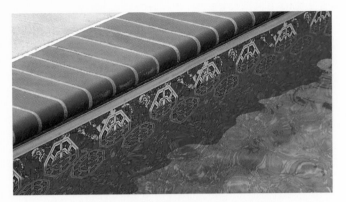

▲ VINYL LINERS OFFER A SMOOTH YET NONSLICK SURFACE AND ARE available in an expanding array of patterns and colors.

▲ AN AGGREGATE FINISH COMBINES MANY DIFFERENT COLORS OF TINY rock particles. The colors and quantities of each particle can be adjusted to vary the overall color.

▲ TINY TILES LAID IN ARCS AND BANDS ADD A DECORATIVE ELEMENT TO this pool. They also clearly mark the location of the steps for safety purposes.

▶ THE DARKER THE FINISH OF THE pool bottom, the more striking the reflections are. Placing a reflecting pool close to dominant architectural features or trees creates an abundance of clearly defined reflections. A pool in open space reflects only the sky.

▼ UPDATING A VINYL-LINED POOL to reflect current styles or the tastes of new homeowners is easy and affordable. Simply drain the pool and replace the liner.

▶ TRADITIONALLY, POOLS HAVE BEEN PAINTED OR PLASTERED in either white or soft colors. However, dark colors—such as blue, black, dark gray, or green—which call to mind natural bodies of water, are gaining in popularity and offer greater reflecting qualities.

STEPS AND BENCHES

▶ HANDRAILS ALONG STEPS ARE AN added safety feature—especially for small children or those who are less stable on their feet. Here, the rail is placed at one end of a series of broad steps that run the width of the pool.

◀ SEMICIRCULAR STEPS ENHANCE THE curving edge of this pool. The steps are formed from concrete and covered in the same plaster finish as the pool's interior.

Don't Skimp on Skimmers

WATER FLOWS INTO A POOL through inlets and out through skimmers to the filtering system. Skimmers also catch debris from the water's surface. They should be placed on the long, downwind side of small pools and at each end of average-size pools. It's a good idea to add a third, centrally located skimmer in large pools or for pools with vacuum systems. Several evenly spaced inlets help prevent bacteria and algae growth.

◀ THESE INNOVATIVELY DESIGNED STEPS LEAD BOTH TO THE POOL AND TO the spa. The blue tile on the risers makes the steps easier to see, which is especially helpful at dusk and in glaring sunlight, as well as for those with limited vision.

▶ THIS POOL HAS TWO TIERS OF STEPS: one set of gunite steps in the water and a second set of adoquin ledger stone steps out of the water.

▶ WADING AREAS AREN'T JUST FOR young children—adults and teens also enjoy relaxing in shallow areas of a pool. Expanding the top step is an easy way to create a lounging area in a pool.

▼ DECKING MATERIALS, SUCH AS STONE or brick, can be used to create pool steps. Pools are chlorinated, so there's no worry about algae buildup making brick or stone steps slippery.

▷ UNDERWATER BENCHES PLACED
beneath a water feature are
always the most frequented
spot in a pool. For pools without waterfalls, the addition of
a long bench along one side of
the pool can be relaxing, too.

▽ THE BEST PLACE TO RELAX IS A COOL AND CONVENIENT
underwater bench, especially when massaging jets
are placed in the adjacent pool wall.

▲ ALTHOUGH MOST POOLS NEED ONLY ONE SET OF STEPS,
a smaller set tucked into a corner can increase
convenience for getting in and out of the water.
This set also provides a place to rest at the deep
end of the pool.

The Pool's Edge

THE STRIP OF EDGING, or coping, where the pool meets the deck is both functional and aesthetic. It forms a tight seal between the pool and the paving so that water doesn't seep behind the pool wall. It offers a handhold for swimmers and serves as a seat for others who wish to dangle their feet in the water. Therefore, a smooth surface that won't snag swimsuits or rough up hands is preferable. The coping also frames your pool visually. A contrasting paving material calls attention to the pool, while similar or natural materials help the pool blend more seamlessly into its surroundings.

▶ A SMOOTH, ROLLED EDGE OFFERS A comfortable handgrip, which is especially desirable in pools with deep sections where swimmers can't easily touch their feet on the bottom.

▼ WHEN EDGING A POOL WITH BRICK, select a smooth finish and a bull-nosed or rolled edge that won't snag swimsuits or rough up hands.

▲ REMOVABLE CAST-STONE COPING PLACED ABOVE AN AUTOMATIC POOL cover provides access to the operating mechanism.

A Band of Tile

THE MOST DIFFICULT PART of a pool to clean is the waterline. In fact, it's commonly referred to as the "scum line" and can easily resemble a bathtub ring. Keeping the waterline clean is a particular challenge in concrete pools, which is why easy-to-clean ceramic tiles are commonly placed just below the pool's coping. Bands of tile also add colorful and decorative accents to any pool.

▶ HERE, THE COPING DOES DOUBLE duty: It both edges the pool and frames a planting bed that visually anchors one corner of a pool.

Coping Options

I N ADDITION TO CHOOSING THE MATERIALS you place around the edge of a pool, you must decide what finished shape those materials will take.

Rolled edges, which are manufactured from concrete, cast stone, or brick, are smooth and slightly upturned to form a good handgrip for swimmers or a comfortable surface for those who wish to sit along the pool's edge.

Bull-nosed stone, cast-stone, or cast-concrete edges, which are flat but rounded on the end, create a classic, low-profile finish.

Thick, rough-cut stone edges are handsome and lend a casual look to a pool. Rough-cut stone edging often echoes the look and texture of nearby stacked-stone walls.

For a clean, modern look, cantilevered edges are a popular choice: the concrete deck runs all the way up to, and slightly overlaps, the pool's edge. This L-shaped overhang creates the illusion that the deck material is thicker than it really is.

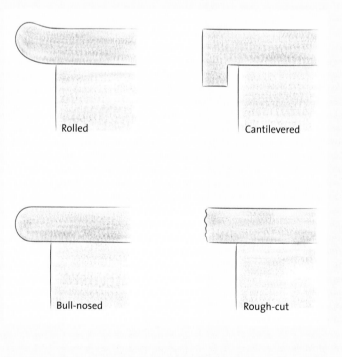

Rolled

Cantilevered

Bull-nosed

Rough-cut

◄ THIS BOULDER, WHICH IS SET INTO THE POOL'S concrete-aggregate edge, provides a comfortable seating place where the homeowners can dangle their feet in the water.

▼ THE CAST-CONCRETE COPING AROUND THIS POOL contrasts with the stained- and stamped-concrete paving and calls attention to the pool's unique form.

THE INFINITY EDGE

▶ WATER CASCADES OVER THE EDGE AND TRAVELS down a series of steps before reaching the catch basin below. The sharp contrast in design between the rectangular pool and the curving basin makes this pool as dramatic when viewed from below as it is from above.

▽ VANISHING-EDGE POOLS—SUCH AS THIS ONE that vanishes on three sides—are at their best when they call attention to scenic views.

▲ PROPERLY PLACED, A VANISHING-EDGE POOL APPEARS TO magically merge with a nearby body of water if the color of the pool's water is carefully matched.

▼ THIS ARCHITECTURAL POOL REFLECTS BOTH THE CONTEMPORARY
lines and modern materials used in the house and looks
dramatic from any angle. Water flows quietly over a
rounded edge.

Creating the Illusion

LTHOUGH THE WATER APPEARS TO VANISH over the pool's edge in an infinity-edge pool, it is actually falling over a structural wall and into a basin or catch pool below the edge, from where it is then recirculated back into the pool. The success of an infinity-edge pool depends on carefully calculated and maintained water levels, solid wall construction (because the wall must support thousands of gallons of water), and a level edge so that the water can flow seamlessly over the wall. Viewed from below the pool, the cascade can be just as impressive as the vanishing edge viewed from above, so this element should be designed as carefully and creatively as the pool itself.

Consider the height of the wall, the surface over which the water falls (which can be a smooth or textured overhang, straight wall, or sloped wall), the size and shape of the basin, construction materials, and access for viewing.

▲ BENEATH EVERY VANISHING EDGE LIES A CATCH BASIN. ON GENTLE SLOPES, WATER MAY DROP only a couple of feet to this basin. On steep slopes, water may cascade down 6 ft. or more, creating the opportunity for a dramatic water feature if viewed from below.

▶ VANISHING-EDGE POOLS REQUIRE A sloping site. The bigger the drop and more open the view, the more theatrical the effect.

◀ WHILE BROAD, SCENIC VIEWS FROM the pool may be breathtaking, a vanishing edge can just as easily call attention to a peaceful garden vignette.

▶ ALTHOUGH AN EDGE WITH A 90-DEGREE angle is most common, vanishing pool edges can take many forms. They can be round, sloped, or overhanging, and water can drop through the air, over a smooth surface, or down a textured surface, such as this stair-stacked stone wall.

NATURALISTIC EDGES

▲ EDGES THAT DESCEND GRADUALLY INTO A POOL, LIKE THE WATER'S EDGE AT THE BEACH, ARE OFTEN REFERRED TO AS "ZERO-LEVEL" ENTRIES. THEY eliminate the need for steps, offer a shallow play area for children, and add to the natural look of a pool. Most zero-level entries are made with sand-textured concrete, but this one features real sand.

◄ NATURALISTIC POOLS REQUIRE THE USE OF NATURAL-looking materials; the use of natural materials, however, doesn't necessarily result in a naturalistic pool. This pool, with its smooth, mortared stones and light-bottomed interior, blends with the landscape but still looks more like a pool than a pond.

▲ IT'S HARD TO TELL THE DIFFERENCE BETWEEN NATURAL and carefully crafted artificial boulders. Artificial boulders can mimic the color, lines, and texture of real boulders—but they weigh much less and can be custom-designed to fit a particular space.

◄ BOULDERS CAN SIT RIGHT AT THE EDGE OF A POOL. Submerging them below the water level gives them a more natural look.

The Pool Deck

WHEN IT COMES TO POOL DECKS, bigger is almost always better. Odds are you'll spend more time around a pool than in it, so you need plenty of space for sunbathing, entertaining, and hanging out with family and friends. When planning your deck, consider both circulation patterns and gathering areas. In addition to the space, which should be scaled to furnishings and activities, you'll want to consider the materials, too. Whether you explore the versatility of concrete or take advantage of the unique virtues of wood, stone, brick, or tile, the materials you choose should be attractive, safe to walk on, and durable in your climate.

▽ WHEN DESIGNING A POOL DECK, ERR ON THE SIDE OF BUILDING one that is too large. This broad deck extends from the house, creating the ideal space for entertaining. There's plenty of room for sunbathing in the chaise lounges, dining at the round table, or mingling with friends on the raised deck during a party.

▲ THE HOUSE, STEPS, AND LOW SEAT wall create a cozy, three-sided nook for dining. In addition, a generous deck surrounding the pool offers plenty of space for sunbathing.

▶ HERE, THE GATHERING SPACE IS SET apart from the pool, making it a destination. The raised pool edge also offers a place to sit.

Making Space

ECKS ARE USED FOR BOTH CIRCULATION and as gathering places. For transitional areas, 4- or 5-ft.-wide decking allows you to move about freely at a safe distance from the pool's edge.

To create a gathering space for lounges, chairs, dining tables, barbeque grills, and such, you can broaden your deck along one or more sides or create an extended patio section in the shape of a square, rectangle, or semicircle. A width of 10 or 12 ft. can accommodate a row of chaises and still provide plenty of pass-through space. A round table with four chairs occupies approximately 9 ft. by 9 ft., while a rectangular table with seating for eight requires 7 ft. by 9 ft. or more. Allow extra space for moving around or for an open-air atmosphere.

Larger decks can accommodate multiple gathering spaces as well as special features, such as fireplaces, barbeque grills, and outdoor kitchen islands.

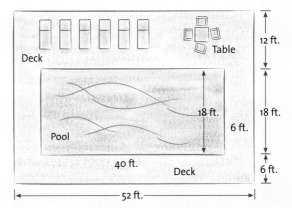

Assembly of chaise lounges and small dining table

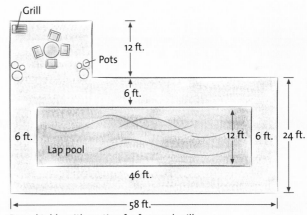

Round table with seating for four and grill

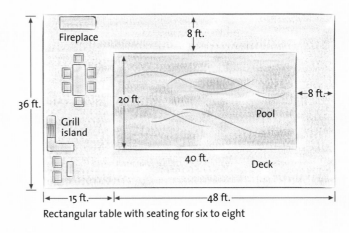

Rectangular table with seating for six to eight

Choosing Decking Material

ECKING MATERIALS ARE CHOSEN PRIMARILY FOR BUDGET AND style preferences. Concrete and wood are the most affordable materials, while cut stone and tile are the most expensive. Even concrete can be affordably upgraded, however, with the addition of brick, tile, or stone bands. By selecting matching or complementary paving materials, you can visually unite your home's architecture with your pool area. A brief description of the advantages of each material follows:

Wood is a popular choice because of its reasonable cost and ease of use. You can choose from domestic woods, such as cedar, redwood, and pressure-treated pine, or imported woods, such as Malaysian red meranti. Keep in mind that you'll need to regularly paint, stain, or seal a wooden deck to maintain its beauty.

Composites are man-made materials that look like wood and may contain a mix of recycled wood, plastics, minerals, polymer resins, or other materials. They cost more than wood, but they resist warping, splintering, rotting, and the wrath of termites better than wood does. Most composite materials do not need to be painted, stained, or sealed.

Poured concrete is one of the most affordable decking options, although it is best suited to warm climates. In extremely cold climates, it may crack. You can finish poured concrete in a variety of colors and textures or stamp it to look like brick, stone, or tile.

Concrete pavers are precast modular units that are available in a variety of shapes, sizes, and colors. You can lay them in a variety of patterns.

Cast stone is a specially formulated concrete that is precast in factory molds and then set in place on-site like stone. It has a clean, classic look. Because it is porous and light colored, it is cooler underfoot than most other paving materials.

Stone comes in a wide range of shapes, sizes, colors, and textures and is one of the most natural decking materials. It costs more per square yard but is virtually indestructible and complements most architectural styles.

Brick lends a traditional look to pools and especially complements homes with brick siding or foundations. It can be laid in a variety of patterns and is easily combined with other paving materials.

Unglazed tile is an elegant choice for pool decks, especially when used both indoors and outdoors to create a unified look. Although most tile comes square, you can find a variety of shapes and sizes.

Concrete

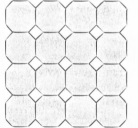

Pavers

Brick

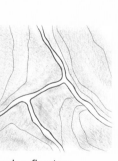

Random flagstone

Tile

Wood

▲ THIS POOL DECK FEATURES BOTH large and small gathering spaces. Multiple gathering spaces are especially useful for families. Parents can congregate in one area while children play in another one nearby.

▶ THE CURVED, BRICK DECK accentuates the arched end of the pool. As long as there is a gathering space on at least one side of the pool, the remaining deck only needs to be wide enough for comfortable passage and accessible enough on all sides of the pool for cleaning.

▲ THIS FREESTANDING RAISED BED ENCLOSES A SEATING area on three sides, creating both a windscreen and a cozy setting that makes the table and chairs a destination for dining, reading, or playing a game of cards. On a warm spring day, the owners could even turn this spot into a home office with a laptop and portable phone.

△ ON STEEP SITES, WOODEN DECKS OFFER A COST-EFFECTIVE ALTERNATIVE TO POURED-CONCRETE WALLS AND decks. The materials are not only less expensive, they also require less engineering and can be easily transported. Choose from among local woods, such as redwood, red cedar, or pressure-treated southern pine; specialty woods, such as Malaysian red meranti or Alaska yellow cedar; or newer manufactured materials such as natural-fiber composites, recycled plastic, or extruded vinyl.

◀ A BROAD BRICK DECK LAID IN A
herringbone pattern creates a
traditional setting around this
pool. The raised deck at the far
end serves as a focal point and
gathering space.

▶ ON A SLOPED SITE, IT MAY BE MORE
convenient to design the gathering space on the same level as the
house or poolhouse. This design
makes it easier to bring food and
beverages outdoors. It's also an
ideal, elevated position from
which to view a pool.

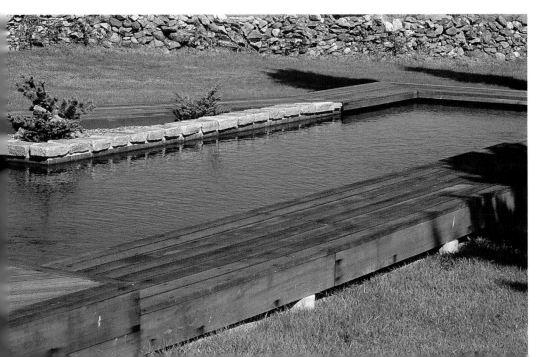

◀ WOOD MAKES A NATURAL-LOOKING
deck and boardwalk. It also combines beautifully with stone, such
as these granite blocks that were
used to create a planting pocket
in one corner.

CONCRETE

▲ CONCRETE CAN BE MIXED WITH
aggregate (small pebbles) for a
brown or gray textured surface
that blends into the surrounding
landscape more naturally than
a standard poured-concrete
pool deck.

▶ LIGHT-COLORED SURFACES FEEL
much cooler to the feet. Cast
stone and terrazzo—both cast-
concrete products with finely
crushed stone additives—are
especially refreshing choices for
hot climates.

▲ CONCRETE CAN BE STAMPED INTO just about any pattern. Here, it is stamped and stained gray to look like cut stone.

Concrete Comes of Age

CONCRETE HAS A NEW LOOK. Poured concrete can now be stained any color; stamped to look like brick, stone, or tile; and brushed or mixed with aggregate to alter the surface texture. Existing concrete decks can be acid-stained or topped with decorative, acrylic floor covering. Concrete pavers—which are available in numerous shapes, sizes, and colors—can be laid in just about any imaginable pattern. They can even be tumbled to give the appearance of old cobblestone.

◄ DOES THIS MATERIAL LOOK LIKE CONCRETE? By stamping and staining concrete, home-owners can achieve the look and feel of stone, brick, or tile at a fraction of the cost.

▼ AGGREGATE ADDED TO POURED CONCRETE VARIES SLIGHTLY in color, allowing homeowners to select a finish that complements the color of their house.

Keeping Cool Underfoot

DARK SURFACES ABSORB HEAT and, on hot days, can be tough on bare feet. Light-colored surfaces are often a better choice around pools, because they reflect the heat of the sun and feel cooler to the touch. Another option for keeping things comfortable is to top your pool deck with an acrylic coating that feels cool underfoot. These acrylic floor coverings can be designed to look like stone, brick, or tile.

▲ EXISTING CONCRETE POOL DECKS in good condition can be dressed up with concrete overlays. Here, an overlay was used to create the look of terra-cotta tile and lightly textured concrete.

▶ IF THE POOL DECK IS LOCATED AT or below the grade of the surrounding landscape, be sure your builder installs a drainage system. Otherwise, rainwater will collect on the deck and run off into the pool.

▲ BLUESTONE HAS A SOFT-TO-THE-TOUCH, smooth finish that is especially desirable around pools. It is visually appealing when laid as irregular or cut stones.

Sorting Out the Stone

THE BEST STONES TO USE for pool decks are flat and smooth but not slick. Stone from local quarries is usually more affordable and blends more easily with your natural surroundings. Stone transported from elsewhere, however, may better suit your architecture. Irregular flagstone lends a casual look, while cut stone imparts a more traditional appearance. Although most pool decks are mortared to keep stones from shifting, the look of dry-laid stone can enhance a natural setting.

▲ THOUGH MOST STONE AROUND
pools is mortared, large, heavy
slabs that are unlikely to shift
underfoot can be dry-laid with
tight joints. Just keep in mind
that uneven surfaces can be
tough on bare feet.

▶ SQUARE GRANITE COBBLES AND
cut-granite-slab coping surround this lap pool for a crisp,
classic look.

▶ LOCAL COMMUNITIES OFTEN
limit the amount of impermeable
surface on a lot. To retain perme-
ability on this site (a good idea
in any location), limestone pavers
were laid in sod, allowing rainwater to soak back into the soil.

▶ STONES VARY IN SIZE AS WELL AS
color and texture. Small stones
tend to create a busy, eye-catching
look. Large stones create a subtler
surface and softer appearance.

△ A SKIMMER-BOX COVER CUT FROM MATCHING STONE blends unobtrusively with the rest of the deck. Don't forget to include a finger hole so it can be easily lifted out.

▷ CERTAIN REGIONS OF THE COUNTRY, SUCH AS THE northeast, have an abundance of natural stone. By using locally available material, homeowners can fashion a pool deck that has a been-there-forever look.

◁ RANDOM FLAGSTONE IS AMONG the most commonly used stone for pool decking. It is available in many different colors and styles, depending on regional availability, and should be mortared in place for stability.

▼ TERRA-COTTA TILE, DUE TO ITS POROSITY, IS ONLY SUITABLE for warm climates. It readily enhances this Mediterranean-style setting in northern California. It would also blend with Mexican- or Spanish-style architecture.

Select a Nonslip Tile

With a long tradition of use around indoor pools, tile is also a tasteful and durable choice for outdoor pool decks. Be sure to select an unglazed yet impervious tile that is intended for exterior use in your climate. Porous tiles tend to crack and flake in cold regions, while glazed tiles pose a safety hazard on decks because of their slippery surface.

▲ TILE CAN BE MIXED AND MATCHED on paving, steps, and wall surfaces. These hand-painted ceramic tiles are set off by the solid, earthy color of the surrounding terra-cotta tiles.

◄ TILE OFFERS GREATER VARIETY THAN perhaps any other deck surface, because it comes in many shapes, sizes, colors, and textures and can be laid in all kinds of patterns. It can be combined with limestone or cast-stone coping and complements stacked-stone retaining walls or raised spas.

▶ TILE WORKS EQUALLY WELL INDOORS and outdoors. For this indoor pool, it is used for the room's walls and for the deck paving. Border and inset accent tiles add a decorative note to this pool deck.

▲ LAY TILES LIKE RANDOM-CUT STONES. BY VARYING THE SIZE, shape, and color, these homeowners created an outdoor flooring that looks like a tapestry.

▲ TILE CAN BE USED TO CREATE OUTDOOR COLOR SCHEMES or to complement color schemes used in the house. Match the color of your interior furniture or walls for a unified look around your pool. Tan and off-white are used consistently throughout this poolscape—right down to the decorative blue tile inset and stripes on the fabric.

◄ THANKS TO ITS UNIFORM APPEARANCE, TILE RANKS among the most formal of all decking materials. Though adaptable to a wide range of settings, it is especially appropriate for classically designed architecture and landscapes.

Landscaping Your Pool

I t's not just a pool; It's a setting. Landscaping around a pool provides a perfect opportunity for you to express your sense of style—whether you are a strict traditionalist, prefer a naturalistic approach, or have a flair for the bold and daring.

One of the first steps in landscaping is creating a sense of enclosure—not just for the privacy it offers but also to create a safe and secure environment. Walls, fences, and hedges also provide a great backdrop for mixed plantings, which add color, texture, and seasonal interest to the landscape and help soften all those hard surfaces around a pool. Lush lawns, clipped hedges, colorful tropical plantings, and broad swaths of ornamental grasses all look equally at home around a swimming pool. Before you pick up a shovel to plant a poolside garden, however, you must first identify the best location for your pool. Select a spot that receives plenty of sunshine, suits the lay of the land, and offers the best views.

Even landscape lighting plays a key role in creating the perfect poolside setting. It improves safety in and around the pool, helps create an inviting atmosphere after dusk, and extends the hours of enjoyment around the pool—whether you're swimming, dining, entertaining, or just relaxing after a long day at the office.

◀ PERFECTLY SITUATED IN THE LANDSCAPE, THIS POOLSIDE SETTING COMBINES SEVERAL IDEAL DESIGN ELEMENTS. THE POOL, located away from shade trees, receives full sun all day. The view from the house is unobstructed. The lawn, wide pool deck, covered terrace, and low periphery plantings provide a balance of shelter, open space, and screening.

Positioning Your Pool

W E'VE ALL SEEN POOLS THAT HAVE BEEN PLUNKED DOWN in the middle of a backyard without much thought or consideration. The most inviting pools, however, are those that settle comfortably into the surrounding landscape and are placed in proper relationship to the house. That's why positioning a pool ranks second in importance only to selecting the right pool. Start by taking stock of the terrain. Look for a site that receives maximum sun exposure and can be easily screened for privacy and security. If it is a naturalistic pool, consider lower-lying areas where you might expect to find a pond. Next, think about how far away you want the pool to be from the house. It can be placed just beyond the back door for convenience, or further away where it serves as a destination or focal point in the landscape. And finally, align your pool to maximize views from the house as well as from the pool deck.

▼ THIS POOL IS POSITIONED AS AN architectural extension of the house. The pool radiates from the staircase, mirroring the lines of the house, with the broad steps continuing right into the pool.

BY PLACING THE POOL CLOSE TO THE house, parents can keep a close eye on children. Proximity also makes trips from the pool to the kitchen and bathroom quick and easy. Because the pool is visible from the house, the surrounding landscape should be designed for year-round interest.

A SHORT, LEVEL PATH LEADING TO the kitchen makes entertaining easy. A more leisurely path (to the right) is designed for strolling. It runs from the living room to the pool by way of a sculpture garden.

BY BUILDING THIS LAP POOL ON A DIAGONAL, THE homeowners gained several feet in length and allowed space for a raised spa. Designing on an angle also makes this small yard appear larger.

THIS NATURALISTIC POOL, TUCKED into the woodland edge, provides a destination for the homeowners. The trees to the north provide a windbreak, and the clearing to the south allows both ample sun exposure and clear views from the house.

RAISING A POOL'S EDGE ADDS dimension to an otherwise flat lot and provides a place to sit. This pool is located in full sun, but a nearby vine-draped pergola offers a shady respite.

◀ VIEWS FROM THE POOL ARE JUST as important as views of the pool. Position decks to take advantage of vistas such as rolling farmland, surrounding hillsides, distant mountains, or natural bodies of water.

Sun and Shade

EXTEND YOUR SWIMMING SEASON by placing your pool in an area where it will receive full sun exposure. The pool water warms up sooner in the summer, remains warm longer as the days of summer wane, and stays a comfortable temperature for swimmers all season long. Nearby shade can be provided by trees, awnings, arbors, umbrellas, or other structures—creating a comfortable environment for those who need a break from the sun's rays or prefer to be near a pool rather than in it.

▲ A BROAD EXPANSE OF LAWN WITHOUT SHADE TREES INCREASES THE NUMBER of hours the sun shines on this pool. It also offers a convenient play area for kids of all ages and acts as a foil for garden beds and borders. A wide deck prevents grass from tracking or blowing into the pool.

▲ NOT ALL HOMEOWNERS WANT TO VIEW A SWIMMING pool from the house, especially if the pool is covered in winter. This one was built on a lower grade and screened by a low hedge to limit views from the living room. It was also designed as a reflecting pool to better integrate with the surrounding gardens.

◀ A TERRACE LOCATED JUST BEYOND THE BACK DOOR HAS a sense of enclosure because the pool is built a few feet above ground level. The terrazzo flooring used inside the house was continued onto the terrace and raised pool deck. The terrace tiles are laid at a contrasting angle to help set the spaces apart.

THE HOMEOWNER CAREFULLY EVALUATED THE natural contours of this property before determining the shape, size, and location of the pool. In the end, a small, round pool was tucked into a curve at a low point in the property. The pool deck is graded in such a way that runoff doesn't end up in the pool after a rainstorm.

BUILDING A POOL ON A STEEP SLOPE IS challenging and requires the expertise of an architect or structural engineer. This pool takes advantage of the grade change by locating a storage room beneath the pool deck.

Show Your Style

SWIMMING POOLS WERE ONCE LITTLE MORE THAN RECTANGULAR HOLES in the ground, skirted by slabs of concrete and broad expanses of lawn. But that's not the case any longer. With so many different pool styles, decking materials, and accompanying poolside structures available, you can create just about any kind of poolside setting you desire.

To pull it all together, you can design stylish landscape and container plantings to complement any style or setting—whether it's a tropical, Southwestern, Mediterranean, naturalistic, or formal theme. For inspiration, take a look at your decorating style, your home's architecture, and the surrounding natural landscape. All provide clues to get your creative juices flowing.

▶ STACKED-STONE WALLS WITH THICK bluestone capstones, white pickets, and teak gates bring a New England–farmhouse style to this poolside setting. The pink roses soften the hard surfaces without hiding the beauty of the textured stone and wood materials.

▲ TIGHTLY CLIPPED BOXWOODS, FLOWERING
hydrangea topiaries, strong geometric
shapes, long axial views, and weathered-
brick paving are all classic design elements used to create a formal setting
in this Southern pool garden.

◄ CALIFORNIA ENJOYS A MEDITERRANEAN-STYLE
climate that is reflected in these poolside plantings. The Italian cypress trees
on the distant hillside add to the setting.

▼ BRIGHTLY COLORED TILE; PRISTINE, WHITE-STUCCO WALLS; AND BOLD-FOLIAGED container plantings are common design elements found in subtropical poolside settings such as Florida and southern California.

▲ COULD THIS BE A LIFEGUARD WATCHING OVER the pool? Well-placed sculptural objects, like the reclining man and the small iron grasshoppers, bring touches of humor to this poolside setting.

◄ THESE HOMEOWNERS CAPITALIZED ON THEIR existing landscape to create a woodland setting. Majestic redwood trees create a dramatic backdrop for this naturalistic pool and give the pool the appearance of being tucked into the edge of a forest.

Unifying a Landscape

TWO KEY FACTORS SHOULD GUIDE YOUR CHOICE OF PLANTS and materials for the poolside landscape: the architectural style of your house and the surrounding natural landscape. Start by choosing construction materials for fences, pool decks, arbors, and other structures that echo the architecture of your home and are common in your region. Stacked-stone walls and wood siding in New England, red-brick paving in the South, and split-rail fencing in the Midwest all help to create a sense of place and determine the style of your poolside setting.

Next, anchor your plantings with native trees and shrubs, or at least plants commonly grown in your region—such as silver-foliaged plants in California, broad-leaved evergreens in the Pacific Northwest, or succulents in the Southwest. To create a cohesive color palette, choose foliage and flowers in colors that echo or harmonize with those inside and on the exterior of your house.

▲ THE ARCHITECTURAL STYLE OF THIS SOUTHWESTERN HOME INFLUENCED THE DESIGN OF THE pool surrounds. Wood details are echoed in the house, arbor, and pool chairs, while the warm hue of the Arizona flagstone harmonizes with the exterior finish of the adobe house. Together, these elements create a strong sense of unity between the house, pool, and landscape.

▲ A DRAMATIC RECIRCULATING
waterfall, loose plantings,
subdued color scheme, and
natural construction materials
such as stone enhance this
naturalistic setting.

Simplifying the Landscape

SWIMMING POOLS AND their accompanying fences, outbuildings, pumps, and accessories tend to clutter a backyard. For this reason, most poolside landscaping should be kept fairly simple in design. With a little ingenuity, landscaping can even help camouflage many of these objects. Here's how:

- Use evergreen trees and shrubs to screen pool equipment and vines to cover fences, arbors, and other structures.
- Limit the number of different hardscaping materials used, selecting those that repeat or complement the materials in your house.

- Plant shrubs, perennials, and ground covers in large masses rather than individually or in small clusters.
- Use dark green as your primary color for shrubbery—it creates a soothing setting.
- Limit your palette to a few colors when planting flowers. Soft, harmonious colors around a pool are more calming than bright, contrasting colors.
- Use garden ornaments with restraint, and place them so they don't visually compete with each other or with the pool structures.

◄ ALTHOUGH THE POOL IS A FAVORITE gathering space, the focus of this backyard is clearly the garden. In fact, the pool is downplayed by a simple design and by positioning the deck so that chairs face the garden. Though the pool itself is not naturalistic in design, a large jump stone helps unite the pool and garden.

◄ THIS CLASSICALLY DESIGNED, crescent-shaped pool sparkles amid the dappled light of a woodland garden. It was built at a lower grade than the house and can be viewed from the patio above. Arching jets seem to transform the pool into a fountain.

Enclosing the Pool

ENCES OR WALLS SURROUNDING A SWIMMING POOL are required in most towns. Even if local building codes don't require them, most homeowners' insurance policies do, as a solid wall or fence that can't be easily scaled will discourage trespassers and prevent unsupervised children from entering a pool. Although 4-foot-high fence requirements are common, a taller enclosure provides the greatest deterrent. In rural locations, where fences may not be required, an impenetrable hedge may satisfy your security needs. Fences, walls, and hedges, however, are more than just barriers. They can improve your sense of privacy, screen undesirable views, provide a solid backdrop for plantings, and surround a pool with warmth and character. A well-crafted wall or fence can greatly enhance the value of your property—especially if softened by attractive vines or used in combination with hedges.

▲ A FENCE OR WALL THAT SURROUNDS A POOL FOR security should be at least 4 ft. high, measured from the outside perimeter. Check local building codes for height requirements of pool fences.

▶ TWO BOUNDARY FENCES SURROUND this pool. The first fence runs the periphery of the property, and the second encloses the pool. The space between the fences provides pets and young children with plenty of room to play and assures parents that access to the pool and the street is secure.

THE HOUSE SERVES AS ONE SIDE OF THIS pool enclosure. It is best to check local building codes before building a pool enclosure—some local ordinances specify that a fence must completely separate a pool from the house.

THE RHYTHM OF HORIZONTAL LINES AND contrasting cutout shapes on this masonry wall complement the architecture of the house. The openings offer glimpses of the natural beauty of the landscape beyond without sacrificing privacy.

▲ THE DARK RED PAINT AND ARCHED WOODEN GATE IN THIS MASONRY WALL DRAW the eye to the far end of the pool and backyard when viewed from the house and patio.

◀ USE GATES AND DOORWAYS TO FRAME enticing views of the pool or surrounding landscape. The iron gates of this entry frame the classical column at the pool's edge. Centering an architectural element in a doorway focuses the eye and signals to visitors that they are entering a soothing, orderly environment.

▲ GROWING VINES ALONG FENCES OR ARBORS IS AN EFFECTIVE WAY TO SOFTEN ALL THE HARD SURFACES COMMONLY found around a pool. An arbor tops this solid-wood fence, providing sturdy support for a climbing wisteria. The slatted roof creates dappled light and allows the air to circulate.

▲ MAKE SURE THAT POOL GATES CLOSE AND LATCH automatically so small children don't wander through doors accidentally left open. Some local building codes require the installation of gate alarms and periphery sensors around the pool area.

Playing It Safe

THE BEST POOL WALLS AND FENCES are high, smooth, and virtually impossible to scale. Although many local building codes may only require a 4-ft. wall or fence, the ideal height for a secure pool enclosure is 6 to 8 ft. Eliminate potential footholds, and close the gaps between fence pickets. Remove any nearby trees or objects that could aid someone trying to climb your fence, and make sure that gates both close and lock on their own. For extra safety, install gate and perimeter alarm systems to frighten off possible trespassers.

◄ THIS INGENIOUS FENCE DESIGN FILLS
many needs. It meets security standards, screens nearby houses, and
keeps overzealous deer from entering
the yard. The lower half serves as a
bench, and the upper half supports
climbing vines. Copper caps on the
finials protect the wood from
weather damage while adding a
decorative touch.

◄ LOW-MAINTENANCE METAL
fencing is readily available,
affordable, and easy to install.
Many manufacturers offer
finishes that do not have to be
painted, and multiple styles are
available to provide an elegant
alternative to the chain-link
fencing commonly found
around a pool.

▶ THIS TALL MASONRY WALL IS
positioned at the end of the
pool for privacy; it screens the
pool from the neighbor's view.
Vine-covered chain-link fencing
placed on a lower grade along
the property's periphery meets
the homeowner's security needs.

◄ SMOOTH, SOLID FENCING IS HARD TO SCALE, SO IT'S IDEAL FOR AROUND A POOL. Although a standard dog-eared privacy fence would do the job, the curved profile and attractive posts of this painted fence add a decorative element to the landscape.

▲ TALL, METAL SECURITY FENCING IS PLACED DISCRETELY AROUND THE PERIPHERY of this property. Landscaping makes the fence almost invisible from the house and pool.

HEDGES

▲ TWO POSTS FLANKED BY DENSE, lush hedges support a decorative iron gate that leads into the pool area. The dark hedges offer an excellent backdrop for seasonal plantings.

▲ HEDGES ALONE MAY NOT SATISFY LOCAL BUILDING CODES, BUT THEY ENHANCE A poolside setting and offer excellent screening. This hedge effectively hides a fence, which keeps young children and pets from entering the pool area unsupervised.

THE LONG HEDGES WORK IN UNISON WITH GATES, FENCES AND A POOLHOUSE to create a sense of enclosure around this pool. The wall of greenery behind the poolhouse increases privacy and offers a solid backdrop for the pool garden.

THOUGH SCREENING IS MOST OFTEN used to hide a pool from view, it is also used to mask unwanted views from the pool. This long, low hedge screens the driveway from view. Because the driveway is a low, flat surface, a higher hedge was not needed.

Poolside Plantings

PLANTINGS ARE ALWAYS A WELCOME SIGHT AROUND THE POOL, whether low-care landscape plants or elaborate garden displays. Plants help soften all the hard surfaces associated with pools and add dimension to an otherwise horizontal landscape. Plantings should look their best in summer to coincide with the swimming season, but other seasons are important, too. Evergreens provide year-round structure and a solid backdrop for flowers, while deciduous plants (those that lose their leaves in winter) call attention to the changing seasons. Flowers, though fleeting, add splashes of color from spring through fall. Including a few fragrant shrubs, vines, or perennials will encourage guests to linger longer around the pool. Contrasting foliage—especially a mix of delicate and bold leaves in varying shades of green, gold, blue, or burgundy—gives the garden long-lasting good looks.

▲ MIXED PLANTINGS AROUND THE POOL SITE HIGHLIGHT SEASONAL CHANGES. HOWEVER, DECIDUOUS trees and shrubs should be placed far enough away from the pool that their leaves, flowers, and berries don't have to be skimmed from the pool's surface or swept from the deck on a daily basis.

When planting to the edge, make sure to use low-maintenance plants that need little pruning and don't produce debris that will drop into the water. Evergreen ground covers are an excellent choice.

▲ A TREE DETERMINED THE PLACEMENT OF THIS poolside patio. The tree provides a canopy of shade for the homeowners when they need an escape from the hot sun.

▲ THESE LARGE EVERGREEN SHRUBS SCREEN BOTH VIEWS AND A CHAIN-LINK security fence. Hollies, laurels, red-tip photinias, yews, or camellias would work equally well to create a similar effect.

▶ BOULDERS ANCHOR THE HILLSIDE above a naturalistic pool, forming planting pockets filled with a variety of ground-hugging and rock-garden plants that thrive with heat and good drainage. Smooth-surfaced boulders offer a casual place to sit near the pool.

◀ NOT ALL TREES PROVIDE SHADE. THESE PALMS WERE PLANTED for their strong architectural lines. As a result, they serve as sculptural elements in the landscape.

create a series of narrow planting beds. These raised beds offer an excellent way to bring fragrant and flowering plants closer to eye level where they can be more closely inspected and smelled. In this landscape, the foliage is just as colorful as the flowers.

Evergreens for Screening

EVERGREEN TREES OFFER AN ADDED LAYER of screening when planted along your periphery. Although they may be small when you plant them, allow ample room for them to grow to maturity. The following trees are excellent choices for a poolside setting:

American arborvitae	*Thuja occidentalis*
Canadian hemlock	*Tsuga canadensis*
Cherry laurel	*Prunus laurocerasus*
Colorado spruce	*Picea pungens*
Douglas fir	*Pseudotsuga menziesii*
English yew	*Taxus baccata*
Foster holly	*Ilex x attenuata 'Foster #2'*
Incense cedar	*Calocedrus decurrens*
Japanese black pine	*Pinus thunbergii*
Japanese cedar	*Cryptomeria japonica*
Leyland cypress	*x Cupressocyparis leylandii*
Redwood	*Sequoia sempervirens*
Rocky Mountain juniper	*Juniperus scopulorum*
Southern magnolia	*Magnolia grandiflora*

▲ FAST-GROWING EVERGREENS, LIKE ARBORVITAE, UPRIGHT JUNIPERS, CYPRESS, OR THESE redwoods, form a dense screen around a pool area in just a few years, blocking undesirable views and increasing privacy.

▲ BROAD-LEAVED GROUND COVERS, LIKE THE PACHYSANDRA shown to the right of this path, provide textural contrast to nearby lawns. Pachysandra is suited to shady areas where lawns would languish.

▶ MIXED PLANTINGS ADD TEXTURE, COLOR, and ever-changing seasonal interest to a poolside landscape. Grow perennials, bulbs, annuals, and flowering shrubs in borders against a wall or fence or in freestanding beds surrounded by lawn.

◄ THIS HOMEOWNER MADE BROAD steps in the gradually sloping lawn that leads from the pool. Rows of granite cobbles mark the steps, which, for continuity, echo the curved lines of the pool deck.

▲ LAWNS RANK AMONG THE HIGHEST-MAINTENANCE PLANTINGS IN THE LANDSCAPE, SO THEY SHOULD BE LIMITED TO WHERE THEY ARE MOST USEFUL as an activity surface or to set off surrounding gardens. Remaining areas can be planted with low-maintenance ground covers. Several flowering and nonflowering species were mixed here to create a garden tapestry.

▲ THIS PLANTING WAS DESIGNED FOR MULTISEASON INTEREST.
Evergreen perennials and ornamental grasses with
sturdy seed heads will stand tall even through the
rigors of winter.

▶ MASS PLANTINGS ARE EASY TO MAINTAIN
and give a landscape a neat and trim
appearance. The fountain grass in the
bed by the pool needs to be cut back
only once a year—in early spring, just
before it puts out new growth.

▲ FLOWERING PLANTS PLACED ON
either side of a path enliven this
passage between the pool and
house. The white flowers contrast with the lush greenery of
the forest setting on the other
side of the pool.

What Not to Plant around a Pool

GROUND COVERS, shrubs, and small trees can be planted
all the way up to the pool's edge and are an excellent way to soften paved surfaces, but many plants make
less-than-ideal poolside companions. As a general rule,
deciduous plants require more work than evergreens
when placed close to a pool. Avoid trees, such as crape
myrtles, that drop lots of flowers, fruits, leaves, and
twigs, or you'll spend the swimming season sweeping
the deck and cleaning the pool filter. Also avoid large
trees with spreading roots that could clog underground
pipes or damage paving. Eliminate flowers that attract
bees, such as mint and bee balm. Barefoot swimmers will
be thankful if you steer clear of prickly plants, such as
hollies and roses, near paths or decks.

▲ THE LAWN WAS REPLACED WITH A MEADOWLIKE GARDEN IN the sunny area just beyond this pool. The garden serves as a more gradual transition between the pool and the woods beyond.

▶ AN ARBOR, DRAPED IN FRAGRANT CLIMBING ROSES, creates a romantic entry into this poolside area, while the fence provides a solid backdrop for a mixed border filled with ornamental trees, flowering shrubs, perennials, and bulbs.

▲ THE GARDEN IS THE STAR OF THIS LANDSCAPE. THE POOL DECK IS KEPT TO a minimum, and a modest patio near the spa offers a place to view both the pool and garden.

Celebrate the Changing Seasons

WHILE EVERGREENS PROVIDE year-round structure in a poolside landscape, deciduous plants celebrate the changing of the seasons. Many deciduous trees and shrubs, as well as perennials and bulbs, offer spring flowers, lush summer foliage, colorful fall leaves, and perhaps even berries or eye-catching bark in winter. Seek out plants with three or more seasons of interest, and place them against a building or evergreen backdrop for the greatest effect.

▲ THE COVERED POOL SIGNALS THAT THE SWIMMING SEASON IS OVER, YET the poolside garden still looks attractive. The evergreen plantings screen the pool from view during the off-season. In summer, the knot garden and arbor create an inviting entry to the pool area.

▲ THE POOL, SURROUNDED ON ALL SIDES BY LUSH BEDS and borders, is the centerpiece of this garden. The gardens ensure a good view from every poolside seating area.

▶ GARDENERS WITH LUSH POOLSIDE PLANTINGS CAN TAKE ADVANTAGE OF THE REFLECTIVE QUALITY OF water, especially if they have a dark-bottomed pool. Flowering tickseed coreopsis spills out over this pool's edge.

▶ A PROFUSION OF PINK AND WHITE FLOWERS CALLS attention to this clover-leaf-shaped garden pool in springtime. Box planters are part of the pool design, and they are filled with flowering azaleas.

▲ LONG-BLOOMING FLOWERS ARE
ideal choices for planting around
a pool. Annuals have the longest
season of bloom, but perennials,
such as these Black-eyed Susans
and tickseed coreopsis, will return
to flower from year to year.

▲ COOL PASTEL COLORS CREATE A SOOTHING POOLSIDE SETTING. THE LUSH PLANTINGS SURROUND
and help soften the curved stone deck that surrounds this pool.

Foliage Plants for Long-Season Good Looks

FLOWERS ARE FLEETING, so plants with attractive foliage give your poolside garden long-season good looks. Try a few of the following workhorse plants in your beds and borders:

Artemisia	*Artemisia* spp.
Banana	*Musa* spp.
Canna	*Canna* cvs.
Cardoon	*Cynara cardunculus*
Coleus	*Solenostemon scuttelarioides*
Hosta	*Hosta* spp.
Japanese silver grass	*Miscanthus sinensis* 'Morning Light'
Lambs' ears	*Stachys byzantina*
Lavender	*Lavandula* spp.
Mexican feathergrass	*Nassella tenuissima*
New Zealand flax	*Phormium tenax*
Spurge	*Euphorbia* spp.

▲ MANY SHADES OF GREEN HIGHLIGHT THE PLANTINGS IN THIS GARDEN TO CREATE AN interesting color palette. They run the gamut from yellow-green to gray-green, to a rich, dark green.

▲ A GARDEN CREATES AN ENVIRONMENT THAT DRAWS people to the pool, even when swimming is not on the agenda. This garden adapts well for entertaining, allowing guests to mingle around the pool or stroll along garden paths without straying too far from the center of activity.

▼ BY BUILDING THIS FENCE ATOP A RAISED BED, ITS HEIGHT WAS INCREASED BY A FOOT or more. Raised beds make plantings easily accessible and also allow for the improvement of soil conditions and drainage in a garden with problem soils.

▲ MANY TREES AND SHRUBS, LIKE THESE hydrangeas just coming into bloom, sport showy blossoms. The neatly trimmed hedges frame each hydrangea to give the poolside an air of formality.

▶ ALTHOUGH A GARDEN BORDER AS wide as 2 ft. will suffice, a 4- to 6-ft. border is better suited to the scale of most pools. A narrow access path along the back of deep borders makes it easier to manage seasonal chores.

PLANTING POCKETS

▶ THESE TWO PLANTING POCKETS, SURROUNDED BY boulders, look like small islands. The dwarf evergreens planted in the pockets flourish, even with their roots confined to a small space. These trees produce minimal debris, so there's no worry about cleanup.

▼ ORNAMENTAL GRASSES, LIKE THIS FOUNTAIN GRASS, WERE a natural choice for planting in pockets around this pool's edge. They enhance the natural setting, produce very little debris, shimmer in sunlight, sway in gentle breezes, and stand tall throughout winter.

▲ BY OMITTING A FEW BRICKS WHEN PAVING THE POOL DECK, PLANTING pockets were created along the edge of this pool. Before planting heat- and drought-tolerant plants, the soil in planting pockets should be amended with organic matter and coarse sand.

▼ SMALL BOULDERS ARE A NATURAL ADDITION TO PLANTING POCKETS AROUND
naturalistic pools and those with random-stone decking. By burying part of the boulders, rather than simply setting them atop the deck or ground, they look more natural.

▼ BECAUSE PLANTING POCKETS ARE
located in full sun and surrounded by large expanses of paving, they create hot, dry conditions for plants. Succulents, rock-garden plants, Mediterranean plants, and many ornamental grasses thrive under these conditions. Even so, they should be watered from time to time.

CONTAINER PLANTINGS

▼ CLUSTER SEVERAL CONTAINERS AS focal points, amid a grouping of lounge chairs or at transitional points such as steps, gates, or corners. This group of pots anchors one corner of the path that leads to the pool.

▶ BLUE POTS ALWAYS LOOK GREAT around a pool because they harmonize with the water color. This ceramic pot matches the tile around the waterline as well.

▲ STRIKING WATER GARDENS CAN BE CREATED IN CONTAINERS. SIMPLY choose a glazed pot without drainage holes, fill it with water, and add several water-loving plants. To support and vary the height of the plants, set them on bricks placed on the bottom of the pot.

◀ POTS CAN BE PLACED ON THE POOL DECK, ATOP RETAINING WALLS, ON tables, near gates, or against a fence. This one anchors the end of a bench that is built into a retaining wall. The vessel's smoky hue and the purple flowers contrast with the terra-cotta bench and white stucco wall.

▼ PLACE SEVERAL PLANTS IN A SINGLE POT TO CREATE A MINIATURE GARDEN. The secret to successful container gardening is combining plants that need similar growing conditions and that won't out-compete each other, yet offer enough contrast in shape, size, and color to be eye-catching. Trailing plants are especially nice for concealing the container's edge.

▼ LONG, NARROW PLANTER BOXES FILLED WITH FLOWERS HELP enclose the pool area by creating a soft, slightly raised barrier along the edge of the pool deck.

▲ TEAK PLANTER BOXES ARE CLASSIC IN STYLE AND WEATHER WELL. SQUARE OR rectangular planter boxes look at home around rectangular pools; the repetition of shapes helps create a sense of unity. This pair of matched planters is host to hydrangeas and trailing vines.

Pots around the Pool

WHEN YOU PLACE A POT IN FULL SUN, the soil can dry out quickly and must be watered daily. One solution is to install a drip irrigation system for your pots and place them on a timer. Another is to use oversized pots, which hold more soil and don't dry out as quickly. Adding compost and a few water-retention crystals to the potting soil helps, too.

△ CONTAINER PLANTINGS BRING A BIT of the tropics to this poolside. In colder climates, like this Connecticut garden, tender plants can be overwintered in a greenhouse or sunny, south-facing room in the house.

▷ FOLIAGE PLANTS, SUCH AS THESE ferns, have long-season good looks and thrive in shady conditions. Two or more plants with contrasting leaf shapes and sizes can be combined to create a striking container composition.

Lighting for Safety and Pleasure

LIGHTING IS ESSENTIAL AROUND A POOL. It not only extends the hours you can spend around the pool, but also makes the pool a safer place after dark. Lighting plays another role, too—that of creating mood and an inviting environment. With the right lighting, you may find that evenings are the most delightful time around the pool. Three major types of poolside lighting are available: General lighting of the pool deck and passageways allows you to move about safely after dark. Underwater lighting enables nighttime swimming and creates special effects in the pool. Accent lighting in the garden, on structures, uplighting trees, or highlighting special architectural features adds atmosphere to any poolside setting.

▲ PATH LIGHTS ILLUMINATE THE STEPS AND THIS POOL DECK. WALL LAMPS AND TABLE CANDLES PROVIDE A MIX OF FUNCTIONAL and romantic lighting on the covered patio. Though these path lights are wired for electricity, wireless solar lights can be added easily to existing poolscapes.

▶ THE LIGHTING AROUND THIS POOL IS layered to be soft and welcoming. Underwater lights allow the homeowners to swim after dark. Uplights placed at ground level accent the pergola and container plantings. Built-in sidelights make the steps safe for passage. And finally, indoor lights call attention to the poolhouse.

▼ UPLIGHTS ADD DRAMA TO THE landscape by highlighting the sculptural qualities of tree trunks and by casting lacy shadows on the walls of the house. Down-lights provide general lighting for the deck and seating areas.

Fiber Optics Shed New Light on Pools

FIBER OPTIC LIGHTING is a safe and versatile option for illuminating pools. Instead of carrying an electric current, the lines that run to underwater fixtures carry only fibers of light. Fiber optic lighting also offers more design flexibility, because it is available in a wide range of styles and colors and can be used to create special effects—such as a kaleidoscope of changing colors or a rim of light beneath the pool's coping. Most existing pool lights can be retrofitted with fiber optic lighting.

▷ GENERAL LIGHTING, AS WELL AS "borrowed light" from the house's interior, brightens the gathering area. Uplights add drama to the setting by highlighting the tree branches overhead.

▽ UPLIGHTS, DOWNLIGHTS, PATH LIGHTS, house lights, and pool lights work together to create an inviting after-dark environment. When illuminated, the house is reflected in the pool.

▲ SMALL PATH LIGHTS ACCENT LOW PLANTINGS AND illuminate pathways around this pool. Fiber optic lighting in the pool gives the water a subtle glow.

◄ THESE HOMEOWNERS TOOK A SIMPLE YET EFFECTIVE approach to lighting. Coach lamps were placed near the home's doors, a single underwater light placed in the deep end of the pool to illuminate the water, and a couple of path lights keep the steps safe. The light from the interior of the house also spills over into the pool area.

Outdoor Rooms and Structures

The most compelling poolscapes include a variety of gathering spaces. Some are open areas designed to remain exposed to the elements. Others are sheltered spaces suitable for year-round enjoyment. There are the in-between places, just beyond the back door, that encourage easy indoor-outdoor living; intermediate areas around the pool that can be used for multiple purposes; and destination spaces that transform backyards into personal retreats running the gamut from porches and patios to pergolas and pavilions. They can be as simple as a garden bench or as elaborate as a poolhouse.

All successful outdoor rooms have several elements in common. They offer a sense of seclusion—even if they overlook grand views. They provide comfortable seating—whether it's a picnic table or cushioned side chairs grouped for casual conversation. Food, beverages, and bathrooms are just steps away—perhaps in the house or a nearby poolhouse. Finally, winning outdoor rooms have character. Their design may be inspired by a home's architecture or interior design, or they may take on a personality of their own in the form of rustic retreats or beautiful garden settings.

Think of an outdoor gathering space as a room with floors, walls, passageways, and ceilings. Create these elements with stone, wood, and brick, and with plants that carpet the ground, soften the walls, or provide a canopy. Add finishing touches by decorating with your favorite colors, furnishing the spaces with weather-resistant furniture, and adding practical amenities such as fireplaces, outdoor kitchens, and water features.

◀ OPENING UP A POOLHOUSE TO LIGHT AND FRESH AIR CREATES A GREATER SENSE OF OUTDOOR LIVING. THIS POOLHOUSE features a dog-trot (pass-through) floor plan with screened double doors that open wide for increased air circulation and views of the pool from either side of the poolhouse.

Gathering Spaces

POOL DECKS ARE THE MOST OBVIOUS PLACE FOR SWIMMERS TO CONGREGATE, but multiple gathering spaces—each a different size and character— can make a backyard more inviting. Open terraces, decks, and patios are favorite places to warm up in the early season, morning, and evening, while shady retreats beneath trees or arbors offer respite from midday and mid-summer heat. Porticos and gazebos, with their solid roofs, are ideal choices in areas where rain showers are common. Such garden structures show up best when painted a light color and positioned against a contrasting evergreen backdrop. Dark or natural-colored structures will blend into the surrounding landscape with ease. If placed along the edge of your property, structures can offer screening and become compelling destinations.

▲ PORTICOS ARE IN-BETWEEN SPACES— not quite outside, yet not quite inside—that are especially conducive to indoor-outdoor living. Tucked into a corner of the house with a roof overhead, this portico offers a cozy, sheltered gathering space that is enjoyable, rain or shine.

▲ A THREE-SIDED PAVILION SCREENS THIS POOL FROM THE NEIGHBOR'S VIEW (AND THE NEIGHBOR'S HOUSE FROM THE poolside view) while creating an intimate space for romantic alfresco dining. Because light colors catch the eye, the painted pavilion is a strong focal point in the landscape.

THE FURNITURE ON POOL DECKS CAN be rearranged from time to time to accommodate special activities or to take advantage of changing sun patterns. This table, set for a dinner party, is positioned to absorb the day's last warm rays of sunlight.

WHEN FACING SOUTH OR WEST, even screened porches benefit from the added shade created by an awning. In this case, the awning also provides rain shelter for a patio dining table. In hot, buggy climates, the preferred dining location shifts between the screened porch and pool deck with the seasons and time of day.

▶ ENCLOSED BY THE HIGH WALLS OF A HOUSE
and hedges, a small terrace overlooking
the pool becomes a cozy spot for a morning cup of coffee or quiet evening escape.
By matching the color and texture of the
terrace paving and fireplace mantle, the
indoors and outdoors are unified by design.

▶ THIS RAISED, OPEN DECK CONVEYS
a different feeling than a small,
enclosed terrace, although both
are conducive to gathering. Such
open spaces are especially suitable for larger groups—whether
family or friends—and tend to
create a more dynamic, energetic
environment. Cozier spaces create a calm, peaceful atmosphere.

Placing Structures in the Landscape

THE FIRST RULE FOR PLACING STRUC-TURES in the landscape is to put them where you think you'll use them. That may sound obvious, but if you place a dining area too far from the kitchen or a gazebo next to the neighbor's compost pile, they'll sit empty. Think about what times of day you want the sun to shine on your structures, how much privacy you need, and how much space is required for activities in and around the structures.

If you're planning for a variety of activity areas and structures, it's often helpful to think in terms of zones by sketching them on a piece of graph paper. For instance, you may want a sunny terrace near the pool for sunbathing; a cozy pavilion in a quiet corner of the lot for candlelit dinners; a small lawn in clear view from the house where young children can play; a shed situated out of sight for stor-

age; and a deck near the kitchen for family dining. Don't forget to include zones for things like circulation, screening, and pool equipment. You may even wish to include zones for elements not directly related to your pool—such as gardens, swing sets, or a dog house. Experiment on paper with several different arrangements before making your final decision.

As you evaluate your site, remember that poolhouses, pavil-ions, and arbors all add a strong vertical accent to the landscape. Place them where you need the most visual punch—either to draw the eye to a favorite part of the yard or away from less desirable views. If you need electricity, water, sewer, or other utilities, make sure you can tap into these lines from your selected site. If you need to bring in large equipment for con-struction, make sure they will have access to the proposed area.

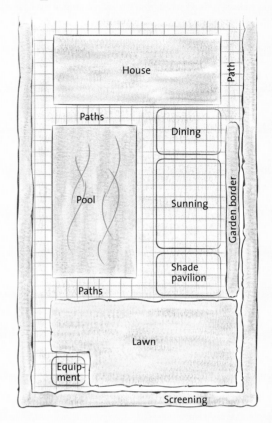

◀ A SMALL GROUPING OF CHAIRS, REGARDLESS of style or arrangement, always issues an invitation to come and sit by the pool for a while. This cluster of Adirondack chairs is sandwiched between large clumps of fountain grass and New Zealand flax at the far side of the pool.

◀ WITH FABRICS DESIGNED SPECIFICALLY
for outdoor use, poolside seating
can be just as comfortable and
decorative as indoor seating. This
homeowner employed a bright
color scheme near the pool with
fabric, paint, decorative accents,
and plantings.

▶ THOUGH TABLES ARE DESIGNED FOR AN
even number of seats, clustering an odd-
number of chairs or chaise lounges on a
pool deck creates a stronger visual statement, inviting casual conversation. These
three comfortable chaises are placed
between the poolhouse and pool,
providing easy access to both the water
and the kitchenette.

◀ BY TUCKING A SINGLE CHAISE LOUNGE AND TINY SIDE TABLE INTO A QUIET corner of the pool deck, this homeowner has declared the space a personal retreat. The chaise is located just steps from the pool and positioned to take in the surrounding views.

▲ RETAINING WALLS CAN TRANSFORM a slope into a seating area. The addition of cushions and pillows makes this masonry and terra-cotta tile wall an inviting place to relax.

◀ LARGE MARKET UMBRELLAS, SUCH AS this oversized model covering a dining table for eight, cast a generous amount of shade. The surrounding stone walls help buffer any unexpected winds that could topple a large umbrella.

▷ RAISED ABOVE THE POOL DECK AND
placed on the distant side of the
pool, this small patio becomes
a compelling destination in
the landscape. Although it is
loosely enclosed, it offers clear
views of both the pool and
surrounding gardens.

▷ LARGE POOL DECKS CAN BE SET UP
to accommodate multiple
gathering spaces. This deck offers
seating, lounging, and dining
spaces along one side. The furniture can be easily rearranged
to accommodate different
types and sizes of gatherings.
In fact, because the furniture is
not too heavy, family members
and guests can do the rearrang-
ing as the afternoon or evening progresses.

Take along a Tape Measure

WHEN YOU FIND YOURSELF IN A COMFORTABLE ROOM, **think** about why you like the space. Estimate the size of the space, note the shape of the room, and sketch the furniture arrangement. Because indoor rooms are great models for outdoor spaces, you can often duplicate an indoor room's layout and many of its features for your pool area. Keep a tape measure and notebook handy for taking measurements and sketching ideas when inspired by other spaces.

◄ A COZY CORNER IS ALWAYS THE FIRST SPOT TO BE CLAIMED BY GUESTS, BECAUSE IT OFFERS A quiet place for conversation and a good view of poolside activities. This one is situated beneath a broad umbrella and tucked between the pool and garden. The planting pocket adds a more complete sense of enclosure.

▼ HOUSE DECKS OFFER A DIFFERENT PERSPECTIVE ON THE POOL. BECAUSE THIS DECK IS convenient to the kitchen and other amenities, it is the preferred gathering space for adults, while the kids tend to spend their time in the pool.

▲ THIS CABANA EXTENDS OUT INTO THE POOL LIKE AN ISLAND. IT HAS A SOLID ROOF (WITH TILES THAT match those on the house) and open sides. Because summer rain is scarce in this northern California community, the curtains are simply a decorative touch.

◀ ATTACHED ARBORS UNITE A HOUSE WITH THE SURROUND-
ING LANDSCAPE. In this case, the arbor covers a platform
deck that overlooks the pool. It is intended as the
only gathering space, a point that is reinforced by
the lack of a traditional pool deck.

▼ MANY ARBORS ARE DRAPED WITH VINES AND PLACED
in an open area to create shade. This one is tucked
beneath the canopy of existing trees to create a
shady retreat for a game of cards, afternoon refresh-
ments, or dinner for four. The raised stone platform
calls attention to the arbor as a gathering place.

Consider Your Climate

YOUR CLIMATE IS AN IMPORTANT DESIGN CON-
SIDERATION. If afternoon showers are
common, a solid-roofed gazebo is more
practical for your pool area than a vine-
covered pergola. If summers are hot,
a north-facing or tree-shaded poolhouse helps you to be cooler under the
scorching sun. If temperatures drop
at dusk, a fireplace allows you to stay
outdoors longer. If you live on an
exposed site, a wall can screen your
dining area from prevailing winds.

▶ COZY SPACES LEND THEMSELVES TO QUIET ACTIVITIES FOR one or two people. When tucked between the pool and a bedroom, they become spaces in which to ease into the day or unwind in the evening. Creating a ceiling overhead—whether from a vine-draped arbor or a canopy of trees—enhances the feeling of privacy and security.

▲ PERGOLAS—EXTENDED ARBORS THAT SERVE AS COVERED pathways or gathering spaces—can run the length of a pool or a building. This one does both—echoing the dimensions of the long, narrow lap pool. The adjacent building features a bar and sink, in addition to a well-disguised, undercounter refrigerator, storage cabinets, and drawers.

▶ THIS RUSTIC ARBOR, FASHIONED FROM WEATHERED LOGS, frames a dramatic view of the pool and the ocean. The rope swing—just wide enough for two— provides the homeowners with a perfect spot to enjoy the sunset while dangling their feet in the water.

All-Weather Furnishings

OUTDOOR FURNISHINGS MUST WITHSTAND the worst of rain, sun, wet swimsuits, and tree litter. In addition to being comfortable enough for lounging, they must be lightweight enough to move around or bring indoors for winter, yet heavy enough to stay in place during a storm. If storage space is at a premium, choose folding or stackable furniture.

The best choices for outdoor furniture include wrought iron and cast aluminum, which resist rust; heavy-duty plastic, which is lightweight and rain repellent; teak and cedar, which weather gracefully; and outdoor wicker, which is actually an alloy frame coated in weatherproof vinyl or resin. Rustic twig furniture looks great outdoors, but even when it's sealed regularly, it has a limited lifespan.

When choosing cushions, select those designed specifically for outdoor use. They should be made from quick-drying foam and covered with fade-resistant, water-resistant, mildew-resistant, and quick-drying fabrics. Choose from among hundreds of fabric colors and patterns to match your style.

▲ THE CUSHIONS ON THESE CHAISE LOUNGES ARE MADE FROM OUTDOOR FABRIC DESIGNED TO REPEL WATER AND dry quickly. The furniture frames are equally durable—just hose them down and wipe them off with a rag if they get dirty.

GAZEBOS OFFER SHELTER FROM SUN AND rain, while remaining open to views and fresh air on all sides. This one is placed at the far end of a swimming pool and painted white, making it a commanding element in the landscape.

ARBORS CAN BE FREESTANDING OR attached to a house. With substantial columns and a high ceiling, this one feels more like a portico (which would have a solid roof). It bridges the gap between the house and pool and supports the natural flow of space between this home's interior and exterior.

THIS LONG AND NARROW WISTERIA-DRAPED ARBOR EXTENDS FROM THE POOLHOUSE TO CREATE A shady dining area around the pool. The retaining wall doubles as a raised-bed planter. The taupe-painted arbor harmonizes with the surrounding California hillside.

AWNINGS AND TENTS CAN SERVE THE SAME ROLE as an arbor or gazebo. This awning continues the color theme of the house, while the fabric provides a soft element to balance the many paved surfaces in this narrow yard.

IN ADDITION TO OFFERING A SHADY SEATING AREA near the pool, this vine-covered arbor, complete with built-in benches, serves as a passageway between the pool deck and surrounding garden. Cushions make the benches more comfortable for sitting.

▲ A FIREPLACE TUCKED INTO THE CORNER OF A PORTICO creates a warm and welcoming roomlike atmosphere while extending the season for indoor-outdoor living. The square tiles laid in contrasting patterns on the face of the fireplace add subtle decorative detailing.

The Sound of Music

MUSIC IS AN ESSENTIAL ELEMENT for the pool area, whether the source is a portable radio or a sophisticated stereo system. A full range of marine-grade, wall-mounted or cabinet speakers are available for use on decks and porches and in poolhouses. Special in-ground units designed for 360-degree sound, along with speakers tightly encased in artificial logs and boulders, blend in with the landscape.

FREESTANDING FIREPLACES CAN be built along with the house or added later. This generously pro-portioned outdoor fireplace is placed in an open area away from the house, where it can equally serve a few friends or a crowd. The extended arbors help to define this area as an outdoor room.

FIRE PITS ARE SMALLER AND MORE affordable than fireplaces, yet they offer similar warmth and ambience. There are dozens of models to choose from, including portable units that burn wood or charcoal and permanent units that use natural gas. Many fire pits are also equipped for grilling.

THIS FIREPLACE IS THE CENTERPIECE OF A WALLED, OUTDOOR ROOM. THE FLAGSTONE fireplace and wall cap match the paving while harmonizing with the stucco. A thick, cut-stone hearth ledge offers a casual place to sit by the fire.

OUTDOOR KITCHENS

▼ GRILLS CAN BE PORTABLE OR PERMANENT AND FUELED BY CHARCOAL, GAS, OR ELECTRICITY. THIS HEAVY-DUTY
charcoal grill is built into a stone retaining wall that doubles as wood storage for a nearby fireplace.
The grill also offers a grilling rack large enough to cook for a crowd.

▲ THIS GRILL IS POSITIONED ON A
terrace above the pool, just
outside the kitchen door. A long
counter provides plenty of serving space, while tiny lights and
an outdoor heater are mounted
to an overhead arbor.

▶ AN INDOOR KITCHEN WITH A
serving window can easily service
outdoor areas. This one also features a counter and bar stools.
The setup offers a creative
solution for serious cooks who
prefer the amenities of a fully
equipped kitchen yet wish to
visit with guests who are enjoying the pool.

▶ A GRILL BUILT INTO A FREESTANDING
island shifts the cooking and
entertaining activities over to the
pool area. With a base of stacked
stone, this island features a smooth
countertop for food preparation
and service and electrical outlets
for a lamp, portable kitchen
appliances, or even a radio.

◄ THIS POOLSIDE PAVILION FUNCTIONS PRIMARILY as a bar, although pool equipment is housed in the basement. There's a pantry in the corner and plenty of appropriate amenities, including a blender, icemaker, and undercounter refrigerator.

▲ THIS BAR COUNTER SEATS FIVE COMFORTABLY. LIKE MANY HEARTY BARS, this one carries out a decorative nautical theme with a captain's wheel, ship's bell, boat lanterns, and marine gauges. Bamboo panels cover the walls, ceiling, and bar base.

▲ A SINK SIMPLIFIES CLEANUP, WHILE UNDERCABINET STORAGE PROVIDES a place to stash pool and party supplies. These countertops— although they are wiped down before use—camouflage the dust and dirt that accumulate outdoors.

Beyond the Grill

OUTDOORS, THE EMPHASIS IS ON GRILLING. To enhance the experience, you can add side burners, smokers, deep fryers, and pizza ovens to transform your BBQ into a full-service outdoor kitchen. Or, you can cook campfire-style over an open fire pit. For safety reasons, keep grills 10 ft. away from seating areas and pools. If you have prevailing winds, consider placing your grill on the downwind side of the pool to limit the smoke in your gathering area.

▷ THIS ROLL-TOP GAS GRILL IS BUILT INTO A CURVING STONE counter that defines one side of an outdoor room. The generous countertop serves a crowd or hosts a collection of favorite potted succulents.

▷ THE EFFICIENCY KITCHEN IN THIS PAVILION CUTS DOWN on the gear that has to be hauled to the pool, because acrylic cups, paper goods, ice, drinks, and snacks can be kept on hand at all times. Simple shelving and undercounter storage help make the most of the space.

Poolhouses

THE LESS TIME YOU SPEND HIKING BETWEEN THE HOUSE AND POOL, the more time you can spend swimming, snoozing, sunning, or socializing. It's hard to beat the convenience of a nearby drink-filled refrigerator, a bathroom that keeps wet feet out of your house, and a simple kitchenette or bar to make serving meals a snap. Poolhouses are the perfect place to stash pool chemicals and picnic supplies and to screen your pool's pump and filter from sight. Position your poolhouse for easy access, to add a vertical accent where needed in the landscape, and to take advantage of the natural light streaming onto your property.

▲ PERCHED ABOVE THE POOL AND WATERFALL, THIS TWO-STORY poolhouse carries through many architectural elements from the main house, such as the colors, construction materials, and woodworking details. The upstairs loft, accessible by a ladder, is carpeted and furnished with floor mattresses and pillows for grandchildren's sleepovers.

▲ A POOLHOUSE IS A SPECIAL FEATURE AND, THEREFORE, SHOULD HAVE CHARACTER. THIS ONE EXUDES coastal New England charm. Though it doesn't feature a large, open gathering space, there's still plenty of room for changing clothes and storing gear. The pool equipment is stored in the back.

▶ THE HEART OF THIS POOLHOUSE IS the gathering room. It remains open to the pool deck, except during heavy rains, when the rolling bamboo blinds can be dropped. The main room is flanked on one side by a bar and kitchenette and on the other by a half-bath.

▶ NEUTRAL COLORS, NATURAL MATERIALS, AND A CEILING fan create a cool, relaxed setting. In addition to the sofa (protected against a far wall), wrought-iron furniture with cushions upholstered in outdoor fabric is used for seating. Light fixtures are also made from wrought iron, as is the baker's rack, which hangs in the kitchenette as shelving.

◀ THE HALF-BATH FEATURES A TOILET AND SINK, AS WELL AS AMPLE ROOM FOR changing clothes. An old basket stores extra rolls of tissue, while the tablecloth hides pool supplies. Old swimsuits convey the decorator's sense of humor and style.

▼ FRENCH DOORS AND A ROOF OVERHANG GIVE THIS POOLHOUSE INDOOR-OUTDOOR
entertaining possibilities in any weather. Arbors extend like wings on
either side, enlarging the available outdoor space. Inside, there's room
for a bathroom, efficiency kitchen, and small living room.

▼ NATURAL LIGHT IS OFTEN THE PRINCIPAL LIGHT SOURCE IN
a poolhouse. If possible, leave windows uncovered
to take advantage of sunlight and garden views.
For increased privacy, choose from curtains, fabric
shades, shutters, or blinds. Or, install frosted-glass
windows, as this homeowner did, to provide privacy
without limiting incoming light.

▶ POOLHOUSES CAN DOUBLE AS GUEST-
HOUSES. Two-story poolhouses can
contain plenty of room upstairs for
a private bedroom. Even in smaller
quarters, sofas quickly convert for
sleeping accommodations. The addition of a small kitchen and bath
make a poolhouse a cozy retreat.

▲ DESIGNED LIKE A WINE CELLAR TUCKED INTO A CALIFORNIA HILLSIDE, THIS POOLHOUSE FEATURES A HALF-BATH, shower, changing room, mudroom, and storage closet where the pool equipment is housed. Arbors flank either side of the building, creating seating and dining areas close to the pool.

FLOOR PLAN OF POOL HOUSE

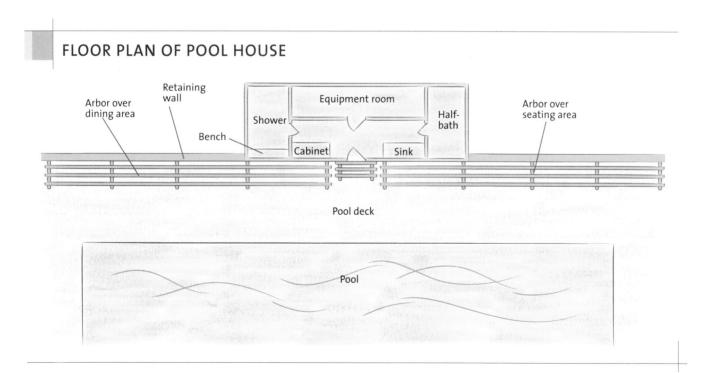

Arbor over dining area

Retaining wall

Bench

Shower

Equipment room

Cabinet

Sink

Half-bath

Arbor over seating area

Pool deck

Pool

▲ A CLOSE-UP VIEW OF THIS POOLHOUSE REVEALS THAT IT HAS been landscaped much like a house would be. A combination of foundation, ornamental, and container plantings frame the building, and flagstone paving covers the terrace, steps, and path that transition into the pool deck.

▲ WHEN PLACING A POOLHOUSE IN the landscape, it's important to consider the views of the building, as well as those from within the structure—especially if it includes seating areas. This one overlooks the pool and landscape and is placed where it is partially screened out of view from the house.

▶ SEATING, DINING, AND GRILLING areas can be located inside the poolhouse, beneath a roof overhang or arbor, or in an open space near the poolhouse. This homeowner opted for a combination of covered and uncovered spaces, using the poolhouse itself for more utilitarian storage and changing rooms.

Storage in the Poolhouse

EVEN SMALL POOLHOUSES **provide lots of storage.** In fact, a bathhouse could be as small as a half-bath in your house and still include shelving over the toilet, a cabinet beneath the sink, stackable bins below a changing bench, and pegs on the wall for towels. Windows and unfinished walls offer ledges for stashing smaller items.

Take advantage of adjustable shelves to make the most of space from floor to ceiling on walls or in closets. In kitchenettes and bars, use pegboard on walls, hanging racks on the ceiling, and under-shelf hooks and racks for cups and wine glasses. Camouflage the storage space beneath counters and sinks with fabric. Fill rooms with practical items such as furniture with drawers. Use antique crates, jars, boxes, baskets, and hampers that can be filled with supplies and easily transported to the poolside. Buy a hat rack for air-drying wet towels and swimsuits.

▲ PORTABLE STORAGE UNITS CONVENIENTLY ROLL OUT ONTO THE POOL DECK during the day, then back in again at night. Carts can be loaded with towels, suntan lotion, snacks, and other poolside amenities. Hampers are ideal for towels headed to the laundry room.

◀ BIG BASKETS, BOXES, OR BINS filled with colorful towels can become decorative elements inside the poolhouse. When swimming, these homeowners move their basket out by the pool for convenience. Attics, antique stores, and flea markets, as well as kitchen and bath stores, are excellent sources for unique containers.

◀ THIS TUDOR-STYLE POOLHOUSE TAKES ADVANTAGE OF A sloped site by incorporating a raised, arbor-covered terrace overlooking a swim spa and gardens. The terrace, though modest in size, offers a seating area for two and a separate dining area for four. Ceiling fans help keep things cool on hot summer days.

▲ POOLHOUSE FLOORS MUST WITHSTAND WET FEET, SO SELECT MATERIALS THAT ARE suited to decks, patios, and terraces—such as stone, unglazed tile, brick, decking materials, or laminates. Cut bluestone is a classic choice that complements the brick façade on this building.

IF CONVENIENTLY LOCATED, A DETACHED GARAGE CAN be transformed into a poolhouse. This one opens up directly onto the pool deck. The pump and filter are located behind the garage and are screened by a fence.

DARK COLORS TEND TO RECEDE INTO THE LANDSCAPE, while natural colors blend in unobtrusively. The dark roof and taupe paint on this poolhouse, along with the narrow, rectangular pool, give the impression that the garden is larger than it really is. In contrast, a white or brightly painted poolhouse and wider pool would make the garden appear smaller.

Open Exposure

POOLHOUSES WITH GATHERING ROOMS are most enjoyable when they open up to the outdoors and let in fresh air. Pocket doors that slide into adjacent walls or French and folding doors that open wide can be locked to secure your poolhouse when it's not in use. Large windows are another option, especially awning-style windows that keep out the rain, even in a sudden shower. If security isn't an issue, you might consider eliminating a wall from one or more sections of your poolhouse. Use shades or curtains made from outdoor fabric or easy-to-clean materials to temporarily close off the interior in a rain shower or during the off-season. If insects are a problem, screening all or part of your poolhouse offers the benefits of fresh air while keeping the bugs at bay.

▲ THIS PAVILION WITHOUT WALLS PUSHES THE ENVELOPE ON THE POOLHOUSE CONCEPT. WHEN WET WEATHER sets in, the curtains are drawn for protection. Curtains used for this purpose can be made of outdoor fabrics that resist water, stains, and mildew or washable fabrics that are easily tossed in the washer and rehung.

◄ ◄ A LACK OF WALLS DOESN'T HAVE TO LIMIT CREATIVITY.
Even without walls, the homeowner has turned the
small space beneath this roof into a combination
open-air bedroom, living room, and dining room.
High ceilings and open walls work together to create
a cool, pleasant atmosphere—even if the ceiling fans
have to provide the breeze.

▼ THIS TWO-STORY POOLHOUSE MAKES EFFICIENT USE OF
limited space on the site by doubling the square
footage under one roof. The brick, stone, and tile
poolhouse also takes advantage of the sloped site.
The multiple levels created by the building and
retaining walls offer many planting opportunities
and viewing platforms.

OUTDOOR SHOWERS

▶ ROT-RESISTANT DECKING, TEXTURED STONE, DECORATIVE concrete, and unglazed tile are all excellent nonslip surfaces for a shower floor. Select a material that harmonizes with your hardscaping or house materials. Here, the shower is conveniently located at one end of a small deck, just steps away from the back door.

▼ IF YOUR OUTDOOR SHOWER IS FOR MORE THAN JUST A quick rinse, both bathers and your neighbors will appreciate a little privacy. Building a complete enclosure around the shower, such as the one shown here, or providing partial screening with panel walls, washable curtains, or dense plantings are all practical ways to screen a shower from view.

▲ OUTDOOR SHOWERS CAN BE EITHER LUXURIOUS WITH ALL THE AMENITIES OR back-to-basics rustic. This one strikes a happy medium with its strategically placed screening panels, wood-plank construction, and exposed plumbing. Regardless of style, a few conveniences, like shelving and towel hooks, make the shower more functional. Shaving mirrors and benches are also appreciated additions in outdoor showers.

▼ OUTDOOR SHOWERS NEED NOT BE ELABORATE. LEAVING THE PLUMBING hardware exposed adds to the rustic outdoor atmosphere and eliminates many of the finishing costs associated with indoor showers. This shower taps existing water lines in the house, further reducing costs and shortening the time it takes hot water to reach the showerhead.

Showering in Nature

ENJOY THE CONVENIENCE and freedom of an outdoor shower. Rinse off after your swim, wash sand and grass clippings from bare feet, or bathe alfresco. For privacy, build a full or partial enclosure. For convenience, include a spigot for a garden hose. For drainage, either tie the shower into your home's sewer line or install a dry well (a deep, gravel-filled pit) beneath the floor of your shower.

▶ EVEN STANDARD UTILITY SHEDS can be dressed up for poolside storage. The oversized doors on this shed improve access to pool equipment, allow more natural light to come into the building when they are opened, and make storing bulky pool furniture at the end of the season easier.

◀ CAMOUFLAGING POOL EQUIPMENT on a small lot always presents a challenge. The designer of this pool area integrated a wood-and-lattice room in one corner beneath an arbor that runs the length of the pool and softened it with plantings. The slatted and latticed sections provide ventilation for the pump, filter, and heater.

◀ A SMALL STORAGE SHED BUILT ON the corner of this wooden pool deck keeps pool-cleaning supplies and recreational gear in one place. Though the structure is strictly utilitarian, it adds a decorative element to the poolscape and is large enough to serve as screening for the pump and filter.

◀ POOL EQUIPMENT SHOULD BE placed close to a pool for peak operating efficiency, but this arrangement creates a landscaping challenge. Though plantings alone could screen the pool equipment, the addition of this sectional fence adds a welcome architectural touch. One panel discreetly doubles as a gate to provide easy access.

Out of Sight

EVERY POOL COMES WITH an assortment of pumps, filters, and, often, heaters. These items should be placed at or near the water level and as close to the pool as possible for the greatest operating efficiency. However, the equipment can be quite noisy, so place them away from your house and as far as possible from gathering spaces. Screen them from view with a small structure, in a closet, or behind a fence, or camouflage them with dense plantings.

▲ EVEN SIMPLE STORAGE BUILDINGS CAN be designed to look attractive. Clean lines, neutral colors, and complementary materials help this building blend into the surrounding landscape. It's helpful to include lighting—inside and outside the building—so that pool equipment and stored items are accessible even after dark.

▲ LARGE UTILITY SHEDS CAN HOUSE POOL EQUIPMENT, POOL CHEMICALS, AND RECREATIONAL GEAR, AS well as garden tools and equipment. Place them behind existing plantings, along the side of a house, or screened from view by trees, shrubs, and vines.

THIS OUTBUILDING ECHOES THE Craftsman-style architecture of the main house. Because it was designed as a utilitarian structure, it is situated along the edge of the property—out of view from the house but not far from the pool. Inside, the building contains changing rooms, a storage room, and an equipment room.

THIS MULTI-PAVILION COMPLEX serves several roles: equipment storage, changing room, and passageway to the pool. Painted blue to harmonize with the pool, the pavilions match the planter boxes placed around the deck.

Resources

Professional Organizations

American Institute of Architects
1735 New York Ave., NW
Washington, DC 20006
800-242-3837
www.aiaaccess.com

American Society of Landscape
Architects
636 Eye St., NW
Washington, DC 20001-3736
202-898-2444
www.asla.org

Association of Professional
Landscape Designers
1924 N. Second St.
Harrisburg, PA 17102
717-238-9780
www.apld.org

Master Pools Guild
www.masterpoolsguild.com

National Spa & Pool Institute
2111 Eisenhower Ave.
Alexandria, VA 22314
703-838-0083
www.nspi.org

Magazines

Pool & Spa Living
860 Pennsylvania Blvd.
Feasterville, PA 19053
www.poolspaliving.com

WaterShapes
P.O. Box 306
Woodland Hills, CA 91365
www.watershapes.com

Pool & Spa News
6222 Wilshire Blvd.
Ste. 600
Los Angeles, CA 90048
www.poolspanews.com

Further Reading

Coventry Pool and Garden House Plans. Manor House Publishing Co., Inc., 2001.

Dream Pools, Deborah K. Dietsch. Michael Friedman Publishing Group, Inc., 2002.

The Essential Garden Book, Terence Conran and Dan Pearson. Crown Publishers, Inc., 1998.

Gardens Are for People, Thomas Dolliver Church. University of California Press, 1955.

Gardening with Water: Fountains, Swimming Pools, Lily Pools, Ponds, and Water Edges, James van Sweden. Random House, 1995.

House Beautiful Pools, Christine Pittel. Hearst Books, 2001.

The New American Swimming Pool: Innovations in Design and Construction, James Grayson Truelove. Whitney Library of Design, 2001.

Pools & Spas: New Designs for Gracious Living, Alan E. Sanderfoot and Jennifer Bartlett. Rockport Publishers, 2003.

Poolscaping: Gardening and Landscaping around Your Swimming Pool and Spa, Catriona T. Erler. Storey Books, 2003.

Reflections on the Pool, Cleo Baldon and Ib Melchior, photographs by Melba Levick. Rizzoli International Publications, Inc., 2001.

Small Pools, Fany Tafari, photography by Pere Planells. Loft Publications, 2001.

The Swimming Pool, Tom Griffiths. Simon & Schuster, 2001.

Swimming Pools & Spas. Sunset Books, 1998.

Credits

pp. ii-iii: Photo: © Robert Stein.

p. v: Photo: © Brian Vanden Brink, Photographer 2004, Design: Horiuchi & Solien

p. vi: (left) Photo: © The Taunton Press, Inc., Design: James Donahue; (right) Photo: © Robert Stein.

p. 1: (left) Photo: © Lee Anne White, Design: Thomas Church; (right) Photo: © Brian Vanden Brink, Photographer 2004, Design: Horiuchi & Solien

CHAPTER 1

p. 4: Photo: © The Taunton Press, Inc., Design: James Donahue.

p. 5: Photo © Alan and Linda Detrick, Design: David Delardi, Landscape Perceptions.

p. 6: Photo: © Tim Street-Porter.

p. 7: (top) Photo: © John Glover/Positive Images, Design: Glen Fries, landscape architect.

p. 8: (top) Photo © davidduncanlivingston.com; (bottom) Photo: © Brian Vanden Brink, Photographer 2004, Design: Mark Hutker Associates, Architects.

p. 9: Photo: © Tim Street-Porter.

p. 10: Photo: © Lee Anne White, House and pool design: Bill Remick, Architect; (bottom) Photo: © Tim Street-Porter.

p. 11: Photo: © davidduncanlivingston.com.

p. 12: (top) Photo: © Roger Turk/Northlight Photography 2004; (bottom) Photo: © Barbara Bourne Photography, Design: Aquatic Technology.

p. 13: (top) Photo: © Tria Giovan, Design: Robert Norris, Architect; (bottom) Photo: © Andrew McKinney.

p. 14: (top) Photo: © Barbara Bourne Photography, Design: Aquatic Technology; (bottom) Photo: © Lee Anne White, Design: Leisure Living Pools.

p. 14: (top) Photo: © Lee Anne White, Design: Atlanta Pools, Inc., Cummings, GA; (bottom) Photo: © Lee Anne White, Design: Leisure Living Pools.

p. 15: (top) Photo: © Alan Mandell, Design: Hendrikus Schravenn, Issaquah, WA. (bottom) Photo: © Lee Anne White, Landscape Design: Paula Refi, Stone Design: Mark Grubaugh.

p. 17: Photo: © Steve Silk.

p. 18: (top) Photo: © The Taunton Press, Inc., Design: John Donahue; (bottom) Photo: © Andrew McKinney, Design: Jack Chandler & Associates.

p. 19: top) Photo: © The Taunton Press, Inc., Design: John Donahue; (bottom) Photo: © Jerry Pavia Photography, Inc.

p. 20: (top) Photo: © Alan Mandell, Design: Clark Matschek, Portland, OR; (center) Photo: © Jerry Pavia Photography, Inc.; (bottom) Photo: © Jerry Pavia Photography, Inc.

p. 21: (top) Photo: © Karen Bussolini/Positive Images, Design: Tramontano & Rowe; (bottom) Photo: © Gay Bumgarner/Positive Images.

p. 22: Photo: © Roger Turk/Northlight Photography 2004.

p. 23: Photo: © Brian Vanden Brink, Photographer 2004, Location: Cape Cod, MA, Design: Perry Dean Rogers & Partners, Architects.

p. 24: (top) Photo: © Andrew McKinney, Design: Jack Chandler & Associates;

(center) Photo: © Alan Mandell, Design: Pamela Burton, Santa Monica, CA; (bottom) Photo: © Dency Kane.

p. 25: Photo: © Brian Vanden Brink, Photographer 2004, Design: John Morris, Architect.

p. 26: (top) Photo: © Robert Perron, Photographer, Design: Joseph T. Sepot, AIA; (bottom) Photo: © Samu Studios, Inc., Design: Keller Sandgren.

p. 27: (top) Photo: © Tim Street-Porter, Design: Arquitectonica Architects; (bottom) Photo: © Brian Vanden Brink, Photographer 2004, Design: John Martin, Architect.

p. 28: Photo: © Lee Anne White, Design: Michelle Derviss.

p. 29: (top) Photo: © Lee Anne White; (bottom) Photo: © The Taunton Press, Inc.

p. 30: (top) Photo: © Jerry Pavia Photography, Inc.; (bottom) Photo: © Karen Bussolini/Positive Images, Design: Lisa Tamm, Landscape architect.

p. 31: (top) Photo: © Karen Bussolini/Positive Images, Design: Johnsen Landscape & Pools, Mt. Kisco, NY; (bottom) Photo: © Tim Street-Porter.

p. 32: (top) Photo: © Karen Bussolini/Positive Images, Design: Johnsen Landscape & Pools, Mt. Kisco, NY; (bottom) Photo: © Gay Bumgarner/Positive Images.

p. 33: Photo: © The Taunton Press, Inc., Design: Connie Cross.

p. 34: (top) Photo: © Tim Street-Porter, Design: Tichenor & Thorpe; (bottom) Photo: © Tim Street-Porter.

p. 35: (top) Photo: © Karen Bussolini/Positive Images; (bottom) Photo: Tony Benner, courtesy Master Pools by Artistic Pools Inc., Atlanta, GA.

p. 36: (top) Photo courtesy Crestwood Pools, Charlotte, NC; (center & bottom) Photo courtesy National Spa & Pool Institute.

p. 37: Photo courtesy National Spa & Pool Institute.

p. 38: Photo: Tony Benner, courtesy Master Pools by Artistic Pools Inc., Atlanta, GA.

p. 39: (top) Photo: © Lee Anne White, Design: Ellis Lan Design; (bottom left) Photo: © Lee Anne White, Design: David Thorne, Landscape architect; (bottom right) Photo: Tony Benner, courtesy Master Pools by Artistic Pools Inc., Atlanta, GA.

p. 40: (top) Photo: © Jerry Pavia Photography, Inc.; (bottom) Photo: © Barbara Bourne Photography, Design: Aquatic Technology.

p. 41: (top) Photo: © Lee Anne White, Design: Richard McPherson, Landscape architect; (bottom) Photo: © Karen Bussolini/Positive Images, Design: Glenn Fries, Landscape architect.

p. 42: (top left) Photo: © Jerry Pavia Photography, Inc.; (top right) Photo: © Brian Vanden Brink, Photographer 2004, Design: Roc Caivano; (bottom) Photo: © Lee Anne White, Design: David Thorne, Landscape architect, Poolhouse: Bev Thorne, Architect.

p. 42: (top) Photo: © Barbara Bourne Photography, Design: Aquatic Technology, Landscape: GardenArt; (bottom) Photo:

© Brian Vanden Brink, Photographer 2004, Design: Mark Hutker Associates, Architects.

CHAPTER 2

p. 44: Photo: © Robert Stein Photography, Design: Cheryl Troxel, Architect.

p. 45: Photo © Lee Ann White, Design: Richard McPherson.

p. 46: Photo: © Anne Gummerson Photography, Design: Laura Thomas, Melville-Thomas Architects.

p. 47: (top) Photo: © Tim Street-Porter; (bottom) Photo: © Saxon Holt/ PhotoBotanic, Design: Thomas Church.

p. 48: (top & center) Photo: © Lee Anne White, Design: Atlanta Pools, Cumming, GA; (bottom) Photo; Courtesy Schwartz and Associates, landscape architects.

p. 49: (top) Photo: © Anne Gummerson Photography, Design: Laura Thomas, Melville-Thomas Architects; (center) Photo: © Alan Mandell, Design: Margaret de haas van Dorsser, Portland, OR; (bottom) Photo: © Jerry Pavia Photography, Inc.

p. 50: (top) Photo: © Lee Anne White, Design: David Thorne, Landscape architect; (bottom) Photo: © Lee Anne White, Design: Michelle Derviss.

p. 51: (top) Photo: © Robert Stein Photography, Design: Barry Sugerman, Architect; (bottom) Photo: © Lee Anne White, Design: Leisure Living Pools, Frisco, TX.

p. 52: (top) Photo: © Lee Anne White, Design: Richard McPherson, Landscape architect; (bottom) Photo: © Karen Bussolini/Positive Images, Design: Johnsen Landscape & Pools, Mt. Kisco, NY.

p. 53: (left) © Lee Anne White, Design: Atlanta Pools; (top right) Photo: © Lee Anne White, Design: Richard McPherson, Landscape architect; (bottom right) Photo: © Lee Anne White, Design: David Thorne, Landscape Architect.

p. 54: (left) Photo: © Lee Anne White, Design: David Thorne, Landscape architect; (right) Photo: © Karen Bussolini/Positive Images, Design: Rolland-Towers Landscape Architects.

p. 55: Photo: © Anne Gummerson Photography, Design: Mike Lehnkering, MSL Associates, Ltd.

p. 56: Photo: © Lee Anne White, Design: Leisure Living Pools, Frisco, TX.

p. 57: (top) Photo: © Lee Anne White, Design: Thomas Church; (bottom) Photo: Tony Benner, courtesy Master Pools by Artistic Pools Inc., Atlanta, GA.

p. 58: (all) Photo: © Brian Vanden Brink, Photographer 2004, Design: Axel Berg.

p. 59: Photo: © davidduncanlivingston.com.

p. 60: © Lee Anne White, Design: Atlanta Pools, Cumming, GA.

p. 61: (top) Photo: Tony Benner, courtesy Master Pools by Artistic Pools Inc., Atlanta, GA; (center) Photo: © Saxon Holt/ PhotoBotanic, Design: Barbara Chevalier; (bottom) Photo: © Lee Anne White, Design: Leisure Living Pools, Frisco, TX.

p. 62: Photo: © Andrew McKinney, Design: Dick Wist.

p. 63: (top) Photo: © Karen Bussolini/Positive Images, Design: Johnsen Landscape & Pools, Mt. Kisco, NY; (center)

Photo: © Jerry Pavia Photography, Inc.; (bottom) Photo: © Andrew McKinney, Design: Jack Chandler & Associates.

p. 64: (left) Photo: © Anne Gummerson Photography, Design: Laura Thomas, Melville-Thomas Architects; (top right) Photo: © Brian Vanden Brink, Photographer 2004, Design: Perry Dean Rogers & Partners; (bottom right) Photo © davidduncanlivingston.com.

p. 67: (top) Photo: © Robert Perron, Photographer, Design: Joseph T. Sepot, AIA; (bottom left) Photo: © Karen Bussolini/ Positive Images, Design: Lisa Stamm; (bottom right) Photo © davidduncanlivingston.com.

p. 68: (top) Photo: © Alan Mandell, Design: Clark Matschek, Portland, OR; (bottom) Photo: © Robert Perron, Photographer.

p. 69: (top) Photo: Tony Benner, courtesy Master Pools by Artistic Pools Inc., Atlanta, GA; (bottom) Photo © davidduncanlivingston.com.

p. 70: (top) Photo: © Roger Turk/Northlight Photography 2004; (bottom) Photo: © Brian Vanden Brink, Photographer 2004, Design: John Colamarino, Architect.

p. 71: Photo: Tony Benner, courtesy Master Pools by Artistic Pools Inc., Atlanta, GA.

p. 72: (top) Photo: © Lee Anne White, Design: Atlanta Pools, Inc., Cummings, GA; (bottom) Photo © davidduncanlivingston.com.

p. 73: (top) Photo: © Lee Anne White, Design: Carrie Nimmer; (bottom) Photo: © Lee Anne White, Design: David Thorne, Landscape architect.

p. 74: Photo: © Tim Street-Porter.

p. 75: Photo: (top) © Brian Vanden Brink, Photographer 2004, Design: VanDam & Renner Architects; (bottom) Photo: © Brian Vanden Brink, Photographer 2004, Location: Martha's Vineyard, Design: Mark Hutker & Associates.

p. 76: (top) Photo: Tony Benner, courtesy Master Pools by Artistic Pools Inc., Atlanta, GA; (bottom) Photo: © Saxon Holt/PhotoBotanic.

p. 77: (top left) Photo: © Lee Anne White, Design: David Thorne, Landscape architect; (top right) Photo: © Tria Giovan; (bottom) Photo: Tony Benner, courtesy Master Pools by Artistic Pools Inc., Atlanta, GA.

p. 78: Photo: © Lee Anne White, Design: Richard McPherson, Landscape architect.

p. 79: (top) Photo: © Lee Anne White, Design: Richard McPherson, Landscape architect; (bottom) Photo: Tony Benner, courtesy Master Pools by Artistic Pools Inc., Atlanta, GA.

p. 80: Photo: © Barbara Bourne Photography, Design: Aquatic Technology.

p. 81: (top left) Photo: © Brian Vanden Brink, Photographer 2004, Design: Thom Rouselle, Architect; (top right) Photo: © Robert Stein Photography, Design: Barry Sugermen, Architect; (bottom) Photo: © Saxon Holt/ Photo Botanic, Design: Brandon Tyson, Pool Builder: Ken Cottrell.

CHAPTER 3

p. 82: Photo: © Lee Anne White, Design: Michelle Derviss.

p. 83: Photo: © Lee Anne White, Design: Michelle Derviss.

p. 84: Photo: © Lee Anne White, House and Pool Design: Bill Remick, Architect; Landscape design: David thorne, Landscape architect.

p. 85: (top) Photo © davidduncanlivingston.com. (bottom left) Photo: © Lee Anne White; Design: Four Dimensions; (bottom right) Photo: © Lee Anne White, Design: Carrie Nimmer.

p. 86: (top) Photo: © The Taunton Press, Inc., Design: James Donahue; (bottom) Photo: © Alan Mandell, Design: Pamela Burton, Santa Monica,CA.

p. 87: (top) Photo: © Anne Gummerson Photography, Design: Mike Lehnkering, MSL Associates, Ltd.; (bottom) Photo: © Lee Anne White, Design: Thomas Church.

p. 88: (top) Photo: © Lee Anne White, Design: Mahan Rykiel Associates; (bottom) Photo: © Lee Anne White, Design: Thomas Church.

p. 89: (top) Photo: © Steve Silk, Landscape architect: Betty Ajay; (bottom) Photo: © Tim Street-Porter.

p. 90: Photo: © Brian Vanden Brink, Photographer 2004, Design: Horiuchi & Solien, Landscape architects.

p. 91: (top) Photo: © Tria Giovan, Design: Ben Page; (bottom) Photo: © Tim Street-Porter, Design: Smith-Miller and Hawkinson, Architects, Akva Stein, Landscape designer.

p. 92: (top left) Photo: © Tim Street-Porter; (top right) Photo: © Lee Anne White; Sculpture: Mavis McClure, Design: Four Dimensions; (bottom) Photo: © Andrew McKinney, Design: Jack Chandler & Associates.

p. 93: Photo: © Tim Street-Porter.

p. 94: Photo: © Alan and Linda Detrick, Design: David Delardi/Landscape Perceptions.

p. 95: (top) Photo: © Alan and Linda Detrick, Design: Cording Landscape Design; (bottom) Photo: © Tria Giovan.

p. 96: (top & bottom) Photo: © Brian Vanden Brink, Photographer 2004, Design: Horiuchi & Solien, Landscape architects.

p. 97: (top) Photo: © Brian Vanden Brink, Photographer 2004, Design: Ron Forest Fences; (bottom) Photo: © Tim Street-Porter.

p. 98: (top) Photo: © Lee Anne White, Design: Carrie Nimmer; (bottom) Photo: © Tria Giovan, Location: Palm Beach, FL.

p. 99: Photo: © davidduncanlivingston.com.

p. 100: Photo: © Dency Kane, Design: Richard Cohen and Jim Kutz, Amagansett, NY.

p. 101: (top) Photo: © Lee Anne White, Design: Michelle Derviss; (bottom) Photo: © Lee Anne White, Design: Leisure Living Pools.

p. 102: (top) Photo: © Karen Bussolini/Positive Images, Design: Johnsen Landscape & Pools, Mt. Kisco, NY; (bottom) Photo: © Lee Anne White.

p. 103: Photo: © Lee Anne White, Design: David Thorne, Landscape architect.

p. 104: (top right) Photo: © Brian Vanden Brink, Photographer 2004, Design: Horiuchi & Solien, Landscape architects; (top left) Photo: © Tria Giovan.

p. 105: (top) Photo: © Dency Kane; (bottom) Photo: © Dency Kane.

p. 106: Photo: © Jerry Pavia Photography, Inc.

p. 107: (top left) Photo: © Karen Bussolini/Positive Images, Design: Johnsen Landscape & Pools, Mt. Kisco, NY; (top right) Photo: © Jerry Pavia Photography, Inc.; (bottom) Photo: © Lee Anne White, Design: Paula Refi.

p. 108: (top) Photo: © Lee Anne White, Design: Thomas Church; (bottom) Photo: © Tria Giovan.

p. 109: Photo: © Lee Anne White, Design: David Thorne, Landscape architect; (bottom) © Lee Anne White, Design: David Thorne, landscape architect.

p. 110: (top) Photo: © Dency Kane, Location: Princeton, NJ; (bottom) Photo: © Lee Anne White, Design: Mahan Rykiel Associates.

p. 111: (top) Photo: © Karen Bussolini/Positive Images; (bottom) Photo: © Lee Anne White, Design: Thomas Church.

p. 112: (top) Photo: © Jerry Pavia Photography, Inc.; (bottom) Photo: © Brian Vanden Brink, Photographer 2004, Design: John Colamarino, Architect.

p. 113: Photo: © Lee Anne White.

p. 114: (top) Photo: © Lee Anne White; (bottom) Photo: © Alan Mandell.

p. 115: (top) Photo: © Steve Silk; (bottom) Photo: © Lee Anne White, Design: Maria von Brincken.

p. 116: (top left) Photo: © Saxon Holt/PhotoBotanic; (top right) Photo: © Jerry Pavia Photography, Inc.; (bottom) Photo: © Saxon Holt/ PhotoBotanic, Design: Thomas Church.

p. 117: (top) Photo: © Karen Bussolini/Positive Images, Design: Johnsen Landscape & Pools, Mt. Kisco, NY; (bottom) Photo: © Dency Kane, Location: Water Mill, NY.

p. 118: (left) Photo: © Tim Street-Porter; (top right) Photo: © Tria Giovan, Location: Nashville, TN, Design: Ben Page; (bottom right) Photo: © Jerry Pavia Photography, Inc.

p. 119: (top) Photo: © Jerry Howard/Positive Images; (bottom) Photo: © Dency Kane, Design: Carol Mercer/Lisa Verderosa.

p. 120: (top)Photo: © Saxon Holt/ PhotoBotanic, Design: Thomas Church; (bottom left) © Lee Anne White, Design: Thomas Church; (bottom right) Photo: © Lee Anne White, Design: Michelle Derviss.

p. 121: (top & bottom) Photo: © Saxon Holt/ PhotoBotanic.

p. 122: (left) Photo: © Alan Mandell, Design: Charyl Butenko, Bellevue, WA; (top right) Photo: © Lee Anne White, Design: Michelle Derviss; (bottom right) Photo: © Saxon Holt/ PhotoBotanic, Design: Brandon Tyson, Pool Builder: Ken Cottrell.

p. 123: (top) Photo: © Lee Anne White, Design: Richard McPherson, Landscape architect; (bottom) Photo: © The Taunton Press, Inc., Design: James Donahue.

p. 124: (left) Photo: © Lee Anne White; (right) Photo: © Dency Kane, Design: Carol Mercer/Lisa Verderosa.

p. 125: (top) Photo: © The Taunton Press, Inc.; (bottom) Photo: © Lee Anne White.

p. 126: Photo: © Barry Halkin.

p. 127: (top) Photo: © Barry Halkin; (bottom) Photo: © Brian Vanden Brink, Photographer 2004, Design: Payette & Associates, Architects.

p. 128: (top) Photo: © Brian Vanden Brink, Photographer 2004, Design: Perry Dean Rogers & Partners, Architects; (bottom) Photo: © Samu Studios, Inc., Design: Jim De Luca, A.I.A.

p. 129: (top) Photo: © Anne Gummerson Photography, Design: Jay Huyett/Studio Three Architects; (bottom) Photo: © Roger Turk/Northlight Photography 2004.

CHAPTER 4

p. 130: Photo: © Brian Vanden Brink, Photographer 2004, Design: Horiuchi & Solien, Landscape architects.

p. 131: Photo: © Lee Anne White.

p. 132: (left) Photo: © Tim Street-Porter; (right) Photo: © Brian Vanden Brink, Photographer 2004, Design: Payette & Associates, Architects.

p. 133: (bottom left) Photo: © Samu Studios, Inc. (right) Photo: © Barbara Bourne Photography, Design: Aquatic Technology.

p. 134: (top) Photo: © Tria Giovan; (bottom) Photo: © Tria Giovan.

p. 135: (top) Photo: © Lee Anne White, Design: Thomas Church.

p. 136: (top) Photo: © Tria Giovan; (bottom) Photo: © Lee Anne White, Design: Richard McPherson, Landscape architect.

p. 137: (top left) Photo: © Tria Giovan; (top right) © Lee Anne White, Design: Richard McPherson, Landscape architect; (bottom) Photo: © Anne Gummerson Photography, Design: Laura Thomas, Melville-Thomas Architects.

p. 138: (top) Photo: © Alan & Linda Detrick, Design: Cording Landscape Design; (bottom) Photo: © Lee Anne White, Design: David Thorne, Landscape architect.

p. 139: (top) Photo: © Saxon Holt/PhotoBotanic; (bottom) Photo: © Lee Anne White.

p. 140: © Lee Anne White, Design: Richard McPherson, Landscape architect.

p. 141: (top) Photo: © Robert Perron, Photograper; (bottom) Photo: © Anne Gummerson Photography, Design: Laura Thomas, Melville-Thomas Architects.

p. 142: (top left) Photo: © Tim Street-Porter; (top right) Photo: © Tria Giovan; (bottom) Photo: © Tim Street-Porter.

p. 143: Photo: © Lee Anne White, Design: David Thorne, Landscape architect.

p. 144: (top) Photo: © Jerry Pavia Photography, Inc.; (bottom) Photo: © Tria Giovan, Design: Sanchez/Maddox Design.

p. 145: (top left) Photo: © Lee Anne White, Design: David Thorne, Landscape architect, Poolhouse Architect: Bev Thorne, Architect; (top right) Photo: © Tria Giovan; (bottom) Photo: © Saxon Holt/ PhotoBotanic.

p. 146: Photo: © Tria Giovan.

p. 147: (top & bottom right) Photo: © davidduncanlivingston.com; (bottom left) Photo: © Tim Street-Porter.

p. 148: (left) Photo: © davidduncanlivingston.com; (right) Photo: © Lee Anne White, House and Pool design: Bill Remick, Architect, Landscape Design: David Thorne, Landscape architect.

p. 149: (top) Photo: © davidduncanlivingston.com; (bottom) Photo: © Dency Kane.

p. 150: (all) Photo: © Lee Anne White, House and pool design: Bill Remick, Architect, Landscape Design: David Thorne, Landscape architect.

p. 151: (top) Photo: © Lee Anne White, Design: Simmonds & Associates, Landscape architects; (bottom) Photo: © Karen Bussolini/Positive Images, Design: Frank J. Gravino, Architect.

p. 152: (left) Photo: © Robert Perron, Photograper, Design: J.P. Franzen Associates Architects, P. C. and Rob Wilbur, OliverNurseries; (right) Photo: © Lee Anne White, Landscape Design: Paula Refi, Stone Design: Mark Grubaugh.

p. 153: (all) Photo: © Lee Anne White.

p. 154: (top left) Photo: © Dency Kane; (top right) Photo: © Tim Street-Porter, Design: Pamela Burton; (bottom) Photo: Tony Benner, courtesy Master Pools by Artistic Pools Inc., Atlanta, GA.

p. 155: Photo: © Lee Anne White, Design: David Thorne, Landscape and poolhouse architect: Bev Thorne, Architect.

p. 156: (top left & right) Photo: © Karen Bussolini/Positive Images, Design: Johnsen Landscape & Pools, Mt. Kisco, NY; (bottom)Photo: © Tim Street-Porter.

p. 157:(top) Photo: © Lee Anne White; (center) Photo: © Lee Anne White. (bottom) Photo: © Lee Anne White, Design: Ellis LanDesign.

p. 158: Photo: © Anne Gummerson Photography, Location Annapolis, MD, Design: Jay Huyett/Studio Three Architects, Landscape Design: Stratton Semmes.

p. 159: (top) Photo: © Lee Anne White, Design: Richard McPherson, Landscape architect; (bottom) Photo: © Tria Giovan.

p. 160: (left & right) Photo: © Tria Giovan.

p. 161: (top) Photo: © Tria Giovan; (bottom) Photo: © Barry Halkin.

p. 162: (left) Photo: © Brian Vanden Brink, Photographer 2004, Design: Mark Hutker Associates, Architects; (right) Photo: © Brian Vanden Brink, Photographer 2004, Design: Steve Foote, Perry Dean Rogers & Partners.

p. 163: (left) Photo: © Brian Vanden Brink, Photographer 2004, Design: Alan Freysinger, Design Group Three; (right) Photo: © Tria Giovan.

p. 164: (top) Photo: © The Taunton Press, Inc., Design: James Donahue; (bottom) Photo: © Lee Anne White, Design: Michelle Derviss.

p. 165: (top) Photo: © Saxon Holt/ PhotoBotanic; (bottom) Photo: © Alan & Linda Detrick, Design: John Van Bourgondien.

p. 166: (top) Photo © davidduncanlivingston.com; (bottom) Photo: © Lee Anne White, Design: Thomas Church.

p. 167: (top) Photo: © Lee Anne White, Design: Thomas Church; (bottom) Photo: © Barry Halkin.